ARABIC
Language and Grammar
Part I

أَللُّغَةُ أَلْعَرَبِيَّةُ وَقَوَاعِدُهَا

تأليف

الدكتور يوحانان كابليفاتسكي

روبين ماس / القدس

ARABIC

LANGUAGE and GRAMMAR

by

Dr. JOCHANAN KAPLIWATZKY

TWELVTH EDITION

RUBIN MASS / JERUSALEM

PREFACE

This book is the first in a series of books which I am about to publish for English students who wish to learn the Arabic language thoroughly and by an easy method.

This book is the result of many years of experience that I acquired in the instruction of Semitic languages generally and of the Arabic language particulary *).

It is the result of the scientific books that I wrote in the Oriental Institute of the Vienna University and in the Semitic-Islamic Institute of the Berlin University.**) and of the Arabic school-books which I published for Hebrew students in Palestine***).

The aim of this book and of those which will follow it is to guide the beginner from the alphabet to a full knowledge of the Arabic language without subjecting him to any undue difficulty and without burdening the grammatical rules with terms and explanations that often cause much difficulty to the layman in matters plilological.

In the very first lesson of this book the beginner will start reading with all the vowels and will go on thus till page 56. It is only there that he will find the list of the Arabic alphabet in its proper order. By then he will have learned all the rules pertaining to correct Arabic reading·

In the pages 1-55 only the lessons 5, 7, 8, 9, 11, 12, 14, 15,

---

*) 1922—1930 in Vienna ; 1931—1933 in Berlin and from 1934 in Palestine.

**) 1. Scientific Grammar of the Arabic Language, 1928

2. Translation of the Hamurapi Laws (from the original) , 1930

3. Scientific Grammar of the Syrian (Aramaic) Language , 1932

4. Translation of the manuscript of the Arabic Commentary on the Mishna of Maimonides (the Tractates Baba-Qama and Baba-Mesi'a) , 1933

5. A dictionary and notes to the philosophical book Dalalat-l-Ha'irin of Maimonides , 1932—3

***) 1. The Arabic Language and Grammar, part I, 1937

(A new edition is under press)

2.   "   "   "   part II, 1938

3. The Arabic Script, 1938

4. The Arabic Verb and its Conjugations, 1938

5. Palestinian Colloquial Arabic, part I, 1939

6. Selected Pieces of the Arabic Press, 1939·

17, 18, 19, 20 and 22 are to be translated from Arabic into English and vice versa; the other lessons in the above pages are only reading lessons and are not to be translated.

From the 57ᵗʰ page onward each grammatical lesson is followed by one, two or three reading lessons composed of texts which are to be translated from Arabic into English and vice versa. The subject matter of these exercises always accords with the preceding grammatical lesson and each of the above texts is followed by an Arabic-English Vocabulary, in which the new words of the text are given

In these vocabularies I often inserted notes referring to the syntax of the Arabic language in order to explain the structure of the Arabic sentence.

At the end of this book an English-Arabic Vocabulary is appended which contains all the words found in the texts that are to be translated from English into Arabic.

Of the verb I have given in this book only the Past and Imperfect (= future and present in the European sense). These were but superficially explained in lessons 11, 17 and 19 in order to facilitate the use of the verb in the texts of this book also. The verb will be fully dealt with in the next book of this series, which is to be published in the very near future.

As a parting word may I draw the beginner's special attention to notes 3 — 5 on page 1 which refer to the correct pronunciation of the Arabic vowels **a, i, u**.

In order to help the student in the study of this book, a key is likewise appended to it.

At the end of this preface I wish to express my sincerest thanks to Mr. Mordecai Zlotnik M.A., at present Programme Assistant (Hebrew Talks) at the Palestine Broadcasting Service, who put at my disposition his wide knowledge of the English, Arabic and Hebrew languages in reading the proofs and in advising me as to the English presentation of the present book.

JERUSALEM,

J. KAPLIWATZKY

Gramatical Contents

First Lesson

(2) (bbb) بيب   (1) (b) ب

(5) (bu) بُ   (4) (bi) بِ   (3) (ba) بَ

(bubabi) بِبَبُ   (bibuba) بَبُبِ   (6) (babibu) بُبِبَ

(bibabu) بُبَبِ   (bubiba) بَبِبُ   (babubi) بِبُبَ

بُبَبِ – بِبَبُ – بِبَبُ – بِبَبُ – بُبَبِ – بِبُبَ

---

(1) The letter **b** (ب) is designated by a point under it.

(2) The letter **b** is written ب   only at the end of a word. But at the beginning of a word, or in the middle of it, it is shortened thus بيب (bbb).

(3) The vowel **a** is pronounced in Arabic like the vowel **a** in the English words : farm, father.

(4) The vowel **i** is pronounced in Arabic like the vowel **i** in the English words : pin, fit, bring.

(5) The vowel **u** is pronounced in Arabic like the vowel **u** in the English words : push, pull.

(6) In Arabic there are three short vowels and three long vowels. The short vowels are :

1. a   بَ   (ba. A small diagonal stroke over the consonant.)

2. i   بِ   (bi. A small diagonal stroke under the consonant.)

3. u   بُ   (bu. The sign ُ over the consonant.)

For the long vowels see page 10 (19).

ت (t) (7)

ت (tu) ت (ti) تَ (ta)

تُتِتَ (tutati) تَتِتُ (tatitu) تُتِتَ (tutita)

تَبُتَ (tubati) بَتُتِ (batuti) تَبُتَ (babuta)

بَتِبَ (tibati) تَتَبُ (tatibu) بَتِبَ (batiba)

بُتَبُ تِبَتُ تُتَبِ بَبتُ تِبَبُ

بَتُبَ ــ تُبَتَ ــ بِبتُ ــ تُتَبِ ــ بُبَبُ ــ تِتُتَ

تُبتَ ــ تِبَتُ ــ بِتُبَ ــ تِتَبُ

ث (th) (8)

ثِ (thi) ثُ (thu) ثَ (tha)

ثَبِتَ (thabuta) بَتثُ (batithu) ثَبِثَ (thabitha)

---

(7) The letter t (ت) is designated by two points above it.

(8) The letter ث is pronounced in Arabic like th in the English words : thank, think.

ثَبُثُ (tithabu) تَثَبَ (bathitu) بَثتُ (thabuthi) ثَبُثِ

بَثتَ (tubitha) بُثتَ (buthita) ثُبِبُ (thubibu) تَبثُ

تَبُبُ بَتثُ تَبثُ ثُبتَ تَبثَ

ثَبُثَ — ثَبُثَ — ثَبتَ — ثُبتَ — بَثثَ — تَبتُ

بَثثِ — تَبثِ — بَثُبَ — ثُبتَ — بُتثِ

(n) ن

(9) (naninu) نَنِنُ

نَبتَ (tubta) تُبتَ (nathibu) نَثبُ (nabata) نَبتَ

تتَبنُ (banat) بنَتْ (tub) تُبْ (tatubna) تتَبنُ

_____

(9) The letter **n** is written ن only at the end of a word. But at the beginning of a word, or in the middle of it, it is shortened thus نَنِنُ (naninu).

(10) Whenever a consonant is without any vowel, it receives the sign ° above it. For example : تُبتَ (tubta), بَنَتْ (banat).

This sign, which indicates the absence of any vowel, is called in Arabic **Sukûn**.

نَبَتْنْ (nabatna) تَشْبْنَ (tathibna) تَشِبْ (tathib)

نَبَتَتْ (nabatat) ثَبُتَتْ (thabutat)

نَثْبُتُ تَنْبُتُ ثُبْتْنَ تَبْنَ تَبْ

تَنْبُتُ ــ نَبَتْنَ ــ بَنَتْ ــ تُبْنَ ــ تُبْ ــ نَبَتَتْ

تَثْبُتُ ــ تَتْبُنَ ــ تَنْبُتُ ــ ثُبْتَتْ ــ تَثِبْ ــ تَشْبْنَ

Second Lesson

 لَلُلِ (laluli) ل (۱) ل

نَبْلُ (nablun) نَبْلٍ (nablin)(۱۱) بَلْ (bal) نَبْلِ

---

(11) At the end of the words, the three vowel-signs are sometimes written double, thus:　ً　ٌ　ٍ . In these cases they are pronounced as if the letter ن (n) was written after them. For example: بِنْتٍ (bintin) تِبْنٍ (tibnin) بِنْتٌ (bintun).

The sign ً is a shortened form of ٌ .

These double-vowel signs ٌ ٍ ً are called in Arabic Tanwin. See page 17 (۴).

(tibnun) تِبْنٌ (12) (lábanin) لَبَنٍ (lábanun) لَبَنٌ

(búlbulin) بُلْبُلٍ (búlbulun) بُلْبُلٌ (tibnin) تِبْنٍ

(thúlthun) ثُلْثٌ (bintun) بِنْتٌ (bintin) بِنْتٍ

بَنَتَ نَبْلٌ نَبَتَ بِنْتٌ بِنْتٍ

بِنْتٌ ــ تِبْنٌ ــ نَبْلٌ ــ لَبَنٌ ــ ثُلْثٌ ــ بُلْبُلٌ ــ

تِبْنٍ ــ لَبَنٍ ــ بِنْتٍ ــ بُلْبُلٍ ــ لِلْبِنْتِ ــ لِنَبَلٍ ــ

لِثُلْثٍ ــ لِبِنْتٍ ــ تَذْنِبُتُ ــ لَبِتَ ــ نَلْبَتُ

ك (k) كُكَكَ (kikuka)

(láka) لَكَ (táktubu) تَكْتُبُ (kátaba) كَتَبَ

(náktubu) نَكْتُبُ (katábta) كَتَبْتَ (kálbun) كَلْبٌ

(bintuka) بِنْتُكَ (taktúbna) تَكْتُبْنَ (náktubu) نَكْتُبُ

---

(12) A small diagonal stroke over the vowel indicates that this syllable is accented

تِبنُكَ (tibnuka) كَلْبُكَ (kálbuka)

كُتِبَ لَكَ كَلْبٍ كَتَبْنَ كَتَبْتُ

نَكْتُبُ ـ تَكْتُبْنَ ـ لَكَ ـ كَلْبُكَ ـ بِنْتُكَ ـ

كَلْبٌ ـ كَتَبْنَ ـ تِبْنٍ ـ كُنْتَ ـ كَتَبْتَ ـ

كَتَبَ ـ بِنْتُكَ ـ لِكَلْبِكَ ـ تِلْكَ .

دُرِرُ (rariru) [13] (r) رُ دِرُ

رَكِبَ (rákiba) تَرْكَبُ (tárkabu) [14] رَكِبْتُ

(kabura) كَبُرَ (bikrun) بِكْرٌ (rakibtu) رَكِبْتُ ... كَثُرَ

(taraktu) تَرَكْتُ (táraka) تَرَكَ (káthura)

· (13) The letter ر (r) is always pronounced in Arabic like **r** in the English words : **r**un, **r**ing.

(14) The letter ر (r) cannot be joined to the following letter. For example : رَكِبَ (rákiba).

تَرَكَ نَتْرُكُ تَرَكْنَ نَرْكَبُ بَكْرُ

كَثُرَتْ ـ نَرْكَبُ ـ تَكْثُرُ ـ رَكِبِينَ ـ تَرَكَبْنَ

كَلْبُ ـ تِبْنٍ ـ تَرَكَ ـ تَتْرُكِي ـ نَتْرُكُ ـ تَتْرُكْنَ

تَرَكْنَ ـ رَكِبَتْ ـ تُبْتْ ـ تُبْنِ ـ تُبْنَ ـ نَبَتَ

نَ (z) زَزِزُ (zazizu)

زُرْتُ (zurtu) (15) زَلْزَلَ (zalzala) زَلْزَلُ تَزُرْنَ

نَزَلَ (nazala) تَنْزِلُ (tanzilu) (tazurna)

زُرْتِ (zurti) تَنْزِلْنَ (tanzilna) زُرْنَ (zurna) زُرْتُ

تُزَلْزِلُ نَزَلْنَ نَزَلْتُ زُرْ كَنَزَ

تَكْنِزُ ـ زُرْتَ ـ تَنْزِلْنَ ـ بَرَزَ ـ تَبْرُزُ ـ تَرَكْنَ

تَرَكْتُ ـ تُرِكَ ـ كَثُرَتْ ـ كَبُرْنَ ـ تَكْبُرُ ـ زُرْتُكَ

نَنْزِلُ ـ زَلْزَلَتْ ـ نَكْتُبُ

Third Lesson

وَ و (w) (16) وُ وِ وَ وو (wawiwu)

ثَوْرٌ (wakala) وَكَلَ (waratha) (17) وَرَثَ

(lawnun) لَوْنٌ (thawbun) ثَوْبٌ (thawrun)

لَوْ (law) ثَوْرٍ (thawrin) لَوْنٍ (lawnin)

وَثَبَ (wathaba) وَزَرَ (wazara)

تَرِثُ لِثَوْرٍ لِثَوْبٍ وَرِثْنَ نَزَلْنَ

ثَوْرُكَ ــ كَلْبُكَ ــ ثَوْبُكَ ــ لَوْنٍ ــ ثَوْبٍ ــ تَرِثُ

تَرِثْنَ ــ تَكْتُبْنَ ــ نَكْتُبُ ــ وَثَبَ ــ وَثَبْتَ ــ تَثِبُ

لَكَ ــ نَثِبُ ــ تَرِثُ ــ لَوْنٌ ــ ثَوْبٌ.

---

(16) The letter و (w) is pronounced like the English **w** in the words: **w**ait, **w**onder

(17) The letter و (w) cannot be joined to the following letter. for example : وَكَلَ (wákala).

ي ‏(ي) (18) يِيِي (yiyuya)

يَرْكَبُ (yárkabu) يَكْتُبنَ (vaktúbna)

يَكْتُبُ (yáktubu) يَرْكَبْنَ (yarkábna)

رَوِيَ (ráwiya) بَيْتٌ (báytun) كَوِي (káwiya)

بَيْتٍ (báytin) يَنْزِلُ (yánzilu)

يَرِثُ يَثِبُ نَنْزِلُ بَيْتُكَ رَوِيتْ

يَتْرُكُ ــ تَتْرُكْنَ ــ يَكْنُبْنَ ــ يَنْزِلْنَ ــ رَوِيتْ
كَوِيتْ ــ يَنْشُبُ ــ نَبَتَتْ ــ بَنَتْ ــ بَيْتْ

م (m) هُم (mimamu)

مِنْكُم (mínkum) بِكُم (bíkum) بَيْتُكُم (báytukum)

رَمَيْتَ (ramáyta) كَتَبْتُم (katábtum) لَم (lam)

مِن (mín) مَرَرْتُم (marártum) يَمْلِكُ (yámliku)

دْميتَمْ زُرْتِ بَيّتٌ زُرْنَ يَمْرَرْنَ

كَتَبْتُمْ – كَتَبْيْنَ – زُرْتُمْ – مَثَلٌ – بَيْتكُمْ

مَرْكَبٌ – وَرَثْتُمْ – تَرَكْتُمْ – رَكِبْتُمْ – تُؤْرِكُمْ

(20) (bābun) بَابٌ (zā) زَا (zū) زُو (zī) زِي

(mā) مَا (zurī) زُورِي (zāra) زَارَ

(19) The long vowels **(**See above page 1 (6) **)** are :

1. ﻱ ِ ا **ī** (i. e. the vowel ِ (i) followed by ﻱ (Y). For example ,

بِي (li) لِي (bī)

2. و ُ **ū** (i. e. the vowel ُ (u) followed by و (w)). For example

يَكُونُ (yakūnu) ; يَزُورُ (yazūru).

3. ا َ ا **ā** (i. e. the vowel َ (a) followed by the letter ا which is called

in Arabic **Alif**). For example كَانَ (kāna) بَابٌ

(bābun).

The long vowels are designated in the English transcription by a horizontal

line above them, for exemple كَانَ (kāna) and are pronounced as follows:

ī like **ee** in **feet**, **ū** like **oo** in **soon** and **ā** like **a** in **rather**.

(20) The **Alif** (ا) cannot be joined to the following letter. For

example بَابٌ (bābun)

(yakúnu) يَكُون (zúrta) زُرْتَ (zúra) زُورَا

(kúni) كُونِي (tháwrī) ثَوْرِي (báytī) بَيْتِي

كَلْبِي يَزُورُنَا زُرْنِي تَزُورُون

تَكُونُ ــ تَكُونُونَ ــ تَكُونِي ــ كِتَابِي

بَابُ ــ بَابِي ــ ثَوْرِي ــ كِتَابُنَا ــ زُورِي ــ نَزَلْنَا

Fourth Lesson

(sasisu) سَسِسُ س (s)

(rassámun) رَسَّامُ (márra) مَرَّ (21) (sállama) سَلَّمَ

(rábbī) رَبِّي (mínnī) مِنِّي (bustánun) بُسْتَانُ

---

(21) The sign ّ above a consonant indicates that the consonant

is doubled. For example سَلَّمَ, pronounce: sállama; شَكّ,

pronounce: shákkun.

Note: سَلَّمَ is pronounced as though written رَبُّ،سَلْلَمَ

= رَبْبُ.

This sign of double consonant (ّ) is called in Arabic **Tashdîd**
or **Shadda**.

سَبَبٌ (sababun) سِتٌّ (sittun) رَبٌّ (rábbun)

مُسْلِمٌ ـ مُسْلِمٍ ـ يُسَلِّمُ ـ سَلِّمْ ـ سَبَّبَ ـ يُسَبِّبُ

يَبَسَ ـ سُمِّيَ ـ سُكَّانٌ ـ سِتُّونَ ـ سَبَبٌ.

شْ (sh) شِشُشَشٍ (shishusha)

شَمْسٌ (shámsun) شَرِيكٌ (sharíkun) (22)

شَرِبْتُمَا (sharíbtuma) شَرِبْتَ (sharíbta) شَرِبْتُ

---

(22) The rules of the accentuation in Arabic are:

1. In words with more than one syllable, the accent is never on the last one.

2. The last syllable but one receives the accent, if the vowel of this syllable is a long one, or if its vowel is followed by a letter with a **Sukun** (°) or with a **Tashdíd** (ـّ) over it. For example مَسْرُورٌ (masrúrun) بُسْتَانٌ (bustánun) كَتَبْتُنَّ (katabtúnna) كَتَبْتَ (katábta).

3. When the last syllable but one does not correspond to the above-mentioned conditions, the accent falls on the last but two, when this syllable does correspond to the above. For example كَتَبْتُمَا (katábtuma); بَنَاهُمَا (banáhuma); يَسُرُّكُمْ (yasúrrukum).

4. In words of four or more syllables the accent is going back to the syllable which corresponds to the above. For

(yárkabuka) يَرْكَبُكَ (mashrúbun) مَشْرُوبٌ

(shubbakun) شُبَّاكٌ (yashrábna) يَشْرَبْنَ

(shubbákin) شُبَّاكٍ (náshara) نَشَرَ نَشَرَبُ شُبَّاكٌ

شَمْسٍ نَشَرْنَا نَمْشِي شَكٌّ

شَرِبْنَا ــ مِشْمِشْ ــ مِشْمِشٍ ــ يُسَلِّمُ ــ يَرْسُمُ

شُكُوكٌ ــ شَرِبْتُنَّ ــ شَمْسٍ ــ يَسْكُتُ ــ نَسْكُنُ

مَشْرُوبٌ ــ نَلْبَسُ ــ سَلِيمٍ

_____

example سَرَرْتُكُمَا (yasúrrukuma) يَسُرُّكُمَا

(sarártukuma).

5. If all the syllables in the word do not correspond to the above-mentioned conditions, then the accent falls on the first syllable. For example كَتَبَ (kátaba); مَكْتَبَتِي (máktabati).

6. The Particles بِ (bi) كَ (ka) لِ (li) فَ (fa) وَ (wa) and hamzat-l-wasl (see bélow page 40 (39)) do not receive the accent. For example بِسَبَبٍ (bisábabin) لِسَبَبٍ (lisábabin) كَسَبَبٍ (kasábabin) وَكَتَبَ (wakátaba) etc.

٨ (h) هِهِهُ (hahihu)

يَهَبُ (yáhabu) وَهَبَ (wáhaba) بَنَاهُ (banāhu)

هَرَبَ (háraba) كَلْبُهُ (kálbuhu) لَهُمْ (láhum)

لَهَا (láhā) لَهُ (láhu) بِهِمْ (bíhim) رَبُّهُ (rábbuhu) رَبُّهُ (rábbuhu)

كَلْبُهُمْ (kálbuhum) كَلْبُهَا (kálbuhā) كَلْبُهَا (kálbuhā)

لَهُمْ لَهَا لَهُ هُنَّ هُمْ هِيَ هُوَ

رَسَّامٌ رَسَمْتُمْ كَلْبُكُمْ هُنَّ

كَتَبَهُ ـ كَرْمُهُ ـ كِتَابُهَا ـ كَلْبُهُمْ ـ كَلْبُنَا ـ بِهِمَا

بِهِ ـ هَرَبَتْ ـ رَاهِبٌ ـ وَهَبَ ـ وَهَبْنَا ـ يَهَبُ

هَلَكَ ـ وَهَبْتُمْ ـ وَهَبْتُنَّ ـ يُسَلِّمُ ـ رَبُّكَ

وَلَدُهُ ـ كَلْبُهَا ـ كَلْبُكُمْ ـ يَكْتُبْنَ ـ دَرَسْنَ

يَدْرُسُ ـ دَرْسٌ ـ دَرْسٍ ـ دَرَسْنَا ـ دَرَسْتُمْ

شَرِبْتُمْ ـ تَرْكِيبٌ ـ مُرَكَّبٌ:

Fifth Lesson
(read and translate)

لِي (li) "I have" لَكَ (láka) "thou (masc.) hast" لَكِ (láki)
"thou (fem.) hast" لَهُ (láhu) "he has" لَهَا (láha) "she has"
لَنَا (lána) "we have" لَكُمْ (lákum) "you (masc.) have" لَكُنَّ
(lakúnna) "you (fem.) have" لَهُمْ (láhum) "they (masc.) have"
لَهُنَّ (lahúnna) "they (fem.) have".

Plural		Singular	
"we have"	لَنَا	"I have"	لِي
"you (masc.) have"	لَكُمْ	"thou (masc.) hast"	لَكَ
"you (fem.) have"	لَكُنَّ	"thou (fem.) hast"	لَكِ
"they (masc.) have"	لَهُمْ	"he has"	لَهُ
"they (fem.) have"	لَهُنَّ	"she has"	لَهَا

<u>Translate</u>: she has; we have; thou (fem.) hast; they (masc.) have; he has; thou (masc.) hast; they (fem.) have; I have; you (masc.) have; you (fem.) have.

(read and translate)

٢. لَنَا بَيْتٌ   ١. لِي بَيْتٌ وَلَكَ بَيْتٌ
كَبِيرٌ   ٣. لَهُ كَلْبٌ كَبِيرٌ وَلَهَا كَلْبٌ كَبِيرٌ

٤. لَهُمْ كَلْبٌ سَمِينٌ وَلَهُنَّ كَلْبٌ سَمِينٌ ٥. لَنَا بُسْتَانٌ كَبِيرٌ وَلَهُمْ كَرْمٌ كَبِيرٌ ٦. لَهَا كَرْمٌ وَلَهُ بُسْتَانٌ ٧. لَكَ بُسْتَانٌ كَبِيرٌ وَكَرْمٌ كَبِيرٌ ٨. كَرْمٌ وَبُسْتَانٌ ٩. بَيْتٌ وَكَرْمٌ ١٠. لَهَا كِتَابٌ كَبِيرٌ وَلِي كِتَابٌ كَبِيرٌ ١١. لَكُمْ كِتَابٌ وَلَهُمْ كِتَابٌ ١٢. لَنَا ثَوْرٌ سَمِينٌ وَلَكُنَّ ثَوْرٌ سَمِينٌ ١٣. لَهُ ثَوْرٌ وَلَكَ ثَوْرٌ وَكَلْبٌ.

Vocabulary: 1. بَيْتٌ "house" 2. وَ "and" (see above page 12-13 (22)) 3. كَبِيرٌ "great"; "big"; "large" (the adjective in Arabic comes after the noun For example: بَيْتٌ كَبِيرٌ and not كَبِيرٌ بَيْتٌ) 4. كَلْبٌ "dog" 5. سَمِينٌ "fat" 6. بُسْتَانٌ "garden" 7. كَرْمٌ "vineyard" 8. كِتَابٌ "book" 9. ثَوْرٌ "ox".

Translate: 1. We have a dog and they (masc.) have a dog 2. He has a big house and she has a big garden 3 They (masc.) have a fat ox and a fat dog 4. They (masc.) have a large vineyard and they (fem) have a big house 5. Thou (fem.) hast a book and we have a book 6. She has a big book and they (fem.) have a big book 7. They (fem.) have a fat dog and I have a fat ox.

Sixth Lesson

د (d) دَدِدُ (dadidu)

وَلَدٌ (wáladun) دَارِى (dári) (23) دَارٌ (dárun)

يَدٌ (yádun) وَلَدَاً (wáladan) وَلَدٍ (wáladin)

كَلْباً (kálban) يَدَاً (yádan) يَدٍ (yádin) يَدِ

كَبِيراً كَرْماً ثَوْراً كِتَاباً بَاباً بَيْتاً

نَارُكَ ـ يَدُورُ ـ دِيكٌ ـ نَارُكُمْ ـ يَدُنَا ـ يَدِي

يُدَرِّسُ ـ دَرْساً ـ دَرْسٍ ـ دَرْسٌ ـ دَرَّسَ ـ وَلَدِي

يَدُكَ ـ يَدِ ـ يَدْ ـ تَدْبِيراً ـ شَرِبْتُمْ ـ تَدْرُسْنَ

يُدَبِّرْنَ ـ دَبَّرَ ـ دَرَسْتُمْ ـ دَرَسْنَا.

---

(23) The letter د (d) cannot be joined to the following letter.

For example وَلَدِي (wáladī).

(24) The **Tanwin** ً (see above page 4 (11)) is always followed by an **Alif** (ا). For example بَاباً (bában) بَيْتاً (báytan).
See below page 33 (36).

ذ (25) (dh) ذَذِذُ (dhadhidhu)

ذَنَبٌ (dhánabun) يَذْكُرُ (yádhkuru) ذَكَرَ (dhákara)

لَذِيذٌ (ladhídhun) كَذِبٌ (kídhbun) (dhánabun)

تَذْكُرْنَ (tadhkúrna) ذُكِرَ (dhúkira) ذَكَرْنَا (dhakárna)

ذَا (dha) تَكْذِيبٌ (takdhíbun) (tadhkúrna)

كَذَّبَ يُكَذِّبُ ذُكِرَتْ تَذْكُرُ

ذُكِرْتُمْ ـ ذُكِّرْتَ ـ كَذَّبْتَ ـ زَارَنِي

زَارَهُ ـ ذَا ـ زُرْتَ ـ رَتَّبَ ـ تَرْتِيبٌ

ف (f) فَفُفَ (fifufa)

دَفَنَ (dáfana) مَلْفُوفٌ (malfúfun) لَفَتَ (láfata)

كَافِرٌ (káfirun) فُلْفُلٌ (fúlfulun) (dáfana)

فِي (fi) فَرَرْتَ (farárta) فَرْدٌ (fárdun)

---

(25) The letter ذ (dh) is pronounced in Arabic like **th** in the English words : **this**, **these**.

مُفْرَدٌ (múfradun)　دُفِنَتْ (dúfinat)

لَفَّ　شَرِيفٌ　شَرِيكٌ　فَكَّرَ　فَرْدًا

فِرَاشٌ ــ فُرْنٌ ــ فَرَّ ــ فَهِمْتَ ــ فِيهِ ــ سَـفِيـنٌ ــ يَفِرُّ ــ مُسَافِرٌ ــ فَرَرْنَا ــ تَفْسِيرٌ ــ كَافِرُونَ .

مَاءٌ (má'un) (26)

شَاءَ (shá'a)　أَكَلَ ('ákala)　أَبٌ ('ábun)

أَنْبَأَ ('ánba'a)　أَبُوكَ ('abúka)　أُكِلَ ('úkila)

إِسْلَامٌ ('islámun)　سُئِلَ (sú'ila)　يَأْمُرُ (yá'muru)

---

(26) The letter ء which is called in Arabic **Hamza** is a click produced by a quick compression of the upper part of the throat. This sound is foreign to English.

But the best way to pronounce it in English is to pronounce every ءُ ءَ ءِ like i a u in the beginning of the English words: is, ill, after etc. For example مَاءِ . بِنَاءِ . pronounce : ma'i .

bina'i (see page 1(4), مَاءَ . بِنَاءَ . pronounce: ma'a, bina'a (see p. 1(3): مَاءُ . بِنَاءُ . pronounce: ma'u, bina'u (see page 1 (5)).

The Hamza (ء) is written sometimes with ا (Alif), some-

يَبْدَأُ (su'álun) سُؤَالٌ (sá'ilun) سَائِلٌ

يَأْكُلُ (yábda'u) (únbi'a) أُنْبِئَ (yá'kulu)

أَمَرَ زَائِرٌ نَبْدَأُ رَأَيْتَ بِنَاءٌ

أَسَرَ ـ أَسِيرٌ ـ أَسْلَمَ ـ يُؤَكِّدُ ـ تَبْدَأُ ـ سَائِرٌ

سَائِلٌ ـ أَرْشِدَ ـ أَكَّدَ ـ أَمِينٌ ـ سَأَلَ.

---

times with ي (y) and sometimes with و (w) or without any

other letter. For example أَكَلْتَ ('akálta) ; بَـدَأَ (báda'a) ;

سُئِلَ (sú'ila) ; يُؤَكِّدُ (yu'ákkidu) ; شَاءَ (shá'a).

Note: 1. When the **hamza** is written with a ي (y), then

the ي is written without its two points. For example

سُئِلَ (sú'ila) هَنِئَ (háni'a).

2. وَ ؤُ ; ئَ ئُ etc. is pronounced 'a, 'u, and

not : wa, wu; ya, yu etc.

3. سَأَلَ. pronounce : sāla; سَأَلَ. pronounce : sá'ala.

4. يَأْمُرُ . يَأْكُلُ . pronounce: yá'kulu, yá'muru,

as if there was a short pause after the first vowel.

Note: The letter ء will be designated in the English transcription by the sign '.

Seventh Lesson
(read and translate)

١. لِي أَبٌ وَأُمٌّ وَلَهُ أَبٌ وَأُمٌّ   ٢. بَابٌ كَبِيرٌ

وَشُبَّاكٌ كَبِيرٌ   ٣. لَنَا بَابٌ كَبِيرٌ وَلَهُمْ شُبَّاكٌ

كَبِيرٌ   ٤. لَهَا دِيكٌ كَبِيرٌ وَسَمِينٌ وَلَهُنَّ دِيكٌ

كَبِيرٌ وَسَمِينٌ   ٥. لَكُمْ ثَوْرٌ سَمِينٌ وَكَلْبٌ كَبِيرٌ

٦. لَكُنَّ بَيْتٌ وَبُسْتَانٌ وَلَهَا كَرْمٌ كَبِيرٌ   ٧. أَنَا

وَأَنْتَ   ٨. أَنْتَ وَهُوَ   ٩. هُوَ كَبِيرٌ وَسَمِينٌ

وَأَنْتَ كَبِيرٌ وَسَمِينٌ   ١٠. لِي فِيلٌ كَبِيرٌ وَسَمِينٌ

وَلَهُ ثَوْرٌ سَمِينٌ   11. لَهَا دَفْتَرٌ وَكِتَابٌ وَلَكِ دَفْتَرٌ

وَكِتَابٌ   12. فِيلٌ وَثَوْرٌ. بَيْتٌ وَبُسْتَانٌ.

Vocabulary: 10. أَبٌ "father" 11. أُمٌّ "mother" 12. بَابٌ

"door"; "gate" 13. شُبَّاكٌ "window" 14. دِيكٌ "cock" 15. أَنَا "I"

16. أَنْتَ thou (masc.) 17. هُوَ "he" 18. فِيلٌ "elephant"

19. دَفْتَرٌ "writing-book"; "copy-book" (Note: هُوَ سَمِينٌ "he is

fat"; أَنَا سَمِينٌ "I am fat"). أَنْتَ سَمِينٌ "thou (masc.) art fat";

Translate: 1. A big door and a big window 2. Thou
(fem.) hast a fat elephant and we have a big and a fat ox

3. I have a copy-book and a book and he has a book
4. She has a fat cock ، 5. We have a dog and you (fem.)
have a dog 6. A father and a mother 7 I and he.
He and thou (masc.) 8 He is fat 9 thou (masc.) art fat
and big 10. You (masc.) have a father and a mother and
we have a father and a mother

Eighth Lesson
(read and translate)

كَلْبٌ (kálbun) "dog"

كَلْبِي (kálbī) "my dog" كَلْبُكَ (kálbuka) "thy (masc.) dog".

كَلْبُكِ (kálbuki) "thy (fem.) dog", كَلْبُهُ (kálbuhu) "his dog",

كَلْبُهَا (kálbuhā) "her dog" كَلْبُنَا (kálbunā) "our dog". كَلْبُكُمْ

(kálbukum) "your (masc.) dog", كَلْبُكُنَّ (kalbukúnna) "your (fem.)

dog", كَلْبُهُمْ (kálbuhum) "their (masc.) dog" كَلْبُهُنَّ (kalbuhúnna)

"their (fem.) dog"

Plural		Singular	
"our dog"	كَلْبُنَا	"my dog"	كَلْبِي
"your (masc.) dog"	كَلْبُكُمْ	"thy (masc.) dog"	كَلْبُكَ
"your (fem.) dog"	كَلْبُكُنَّ	"thy (fem.) dog"	كَلْبُكِ
"their (masc.) dog"	كَلْبُهُمْ	"his dog"	كَلْبُهُ
"their (fem.) dog"	كَلْبُهُنَّ	"her dog"	كَلْبُهَا

Translate: Thy (masc.) dog; our dog; his dog; their (masc.) dog; their (fem.) dog; her dog; my dog; thy (fem.) dog; their (fem.) dog; your (masc.) dog.

Declinate the following two nouns:

"house" بَيْتٌ   "book" كِتَابٌ

"my house" بَيْتِي   "my book" كِتَابِي

"thy (masc.) house" بَيْتُكَ   "thy (masc.) book" كِتَابُكَ

etc.   etc.

and also:

بُسْتَان "vineyard"، كَرْم "gate"; "door" ثَوْر "ox"، بَاب

"garden" فِيل "elephant".

Ninth Lesson
(read and translate)

١. لِي أَرْنَبٌ وَلَكَ أَرْنَبٌ   ٢. أَرْنَبُكَ أَكْبَرُ

مِنْ أَرْنَبِي   ٣. لَهُ كَلْبٌ وَلِي كَلْبٌ   ٤. كَلْبُهُ

أَسْمَنُ مِنْ كَلْبِي   ٥. سَلِيم وَلَدٌ كَبِيرٌ   ٦. شَاكِرٌ

تِلْمِيذٌ كَبِيرٌ   ٧. سَلِيم أَكْبَرُ مِنْ تِلْمِيذِي

٨. شَاكِرٌ أَكْبَرُ مِنْ وَلَدِي   ٩. أَيْنَ ثَوْرُكَ ؟ —

ثَوْرِي فِي بُسْتَانِي   ١٠. كِتَابُكَ أَكْبَرُ مِنْ كِتَابِي

11. كَرْمُهَا أَكْبَرُ مِنْ كَرْمِي   12. ثَوْرُهُ أَكْبَرُ

وَأَسْمَنُ مِنْ ثَوْرِي   13. ثَوْرُكَ وَكَلْبُكَ فِي بُسْتَانِي

14. أَيْنَ تِلْمِيذُكَ ؟ – تِلْمِيذِي فِي كَرْمِي   15. بَيْتُهُ

أَكْبَرُ مِنْ بَيْتِي   16. أَيْنَ أَرْنَبِي ؟ – أَرْنَبُكَ فِي

كَرْمِي .

Vocabulary:

20. أَرْنَبٌ "hare" 21. مِنْ "from"; "of"

22. أَكْبَرُ مِنْ "greater (bigger) than" (كَبِيرٌ "great"; "big")

23. أَسْمَنُ مِنْ "fatter than" (سَمِينٌ "fat") 24. سَلِيمٌ "Salim"

(proper noun masculine) 25 شَاكِرٌ "Shakir"(proper noun masculine)

26. وَلَدٌ "boy" 27. تِلْمِيذٌ "pupil" (سَلِيمٌ وَلَدٌ كَبِيرٌ "Salim

(is) a big boy" شَاكِرٌ وَلَدٌ كَبِيرٌ "Shakir (is) a big boy").

28. أَيْنَ "where" 29. فِي "in".

Translate:

1. His dog is fatter than my dog.
2. Where is their (masc.) ox ? – their ox is in my garden.
3. Her cock is fatter than my cock   4. Thy (masc.) hare is in my garden   5. His boy is bigger than my boy   6. Where is my pupil and thy (masc.) pupil? — my pupil and thy (masc.) pupil are in my vineyard   7. I have an ox and she has an ox. Her ox is bigger and fatter than my ox   8. Where is our dog? — Your (masc.) dog is in my house.

Tenth Lesson

ق (q) (27) قُقَقِ (qiquqa)

يَقُولُ (yaqúlu) قَالَ (qála) قَدَّسَ (qáddasa) قَدَّسَ

قَبْلَ (daqíqun) دَقِيقٌ (yuqáddisu) يُقَدِّسُ

قُوم (yaqúmu) يَقُومُ (qáma) قَامَ (qábla)

شَقَّ دَقَّ قَامَتْ قُلْنَا رَفِيقٌ

شَقِيقٌ ـ أَسْوَاقٌ ـ قُمْنَا ـ قُولِي ـ قَلِيلٌ ـ سُوقٌ

فَرِيقٌ ـ تَقْرَئِينَ ـ يَقْرَأُ ـ قَرَأَتْ ـ قَرَأَ ـ قَنَابِلُ

ج (g) (28) جِجُجَ (gíguga)

رِجْلٌ (gámalun) جَمَلٌ (gísmun) جِسْمٌ

(magnúnun) مَجْنُونٌ (tárgama) تَرْجِمْ (ríglun) رِجْلٌ

---

(27) The letter ق is a **k** sound produced in the throat. In the English transcription it will be designated by **q**.

(28) The letter ج (g) is pronounced like the **j** and like the **g** in the English words: joy and gentle. In the English transcription it will be designated by **ğ**.

حَدِيدٌ (gadidun) جَلَسَ (gálasa)

تَاجِرٌ جَمَلِي بِجَانِبٍ يَجْلِسُ

جَنُوبٌ ـ جَرَّ ـ نَجْلِسُ ـ جَالِسٌ ـ مَاجَ ـ هَاجَ ـ

ثَلْجٌ ـ جَمَلِي ـ لِجِسْمِي ـ تَرْجَمَتْ ـ جِسْمُكَ ـ

جَدٌّ ـ جَدَّتِي ـ جَلَسْنَا ـ جَلَسْتُمْ ـ جَرَّتْ.

ح (h) (29) حِحُحَ (hihuha)

لَحْمٌ (láhmun) حَكِيمٌ (hakimun) بَحْرٌ (báhrun)

رَحِيمٌ (rahimun) مَرَجٌ (márgun) سَلَّحَ (sállaha)

حَلِيبٌ (halibun) وَاحِدٌ (wáhidun)

حَمَلَتْ حِمَارٌ سِلَاحٌ رَاحَ رَحِمَ

---

(29) The letter ح (h) is a consonant which usually gives much
trouble to English students. It is a strong aspirated **h**
produced with effort.

In the English transcription it will be designated by **h**.

حَارِسٌ ـ لَحْمٌ ـ لَحْمُكَ ـ وَاحِدٌ ـ يَحْرُسُونَ

مَرْحُومٌ ـ تَحْتَ ـ حَرَكَاتٌ ـ مِلْحٌ ـ حَرْبٌ ـ نَجَاحٌ

يَحْمِلُ ـ حَدَّثَ ـ حَوَادِثُ.

(30) (kh) خ

خَمْس (yákhruǧu) يَخْرُجُ (kháraga) خَرَجَ

(khámsun) خَبَر (dakhálta) دَخَلْتَ (khábarun)

لَكِنَّ (hádhā) هٰذَا (31) (khámsin) خَمْسٍ

('ibrāhīmu) إِبْرٰهِيمُ ('ilāhun) إِلٰهٌ (lákinna)

خُبْزٌ خَمْسُونَ دَخَلْنَا لَكِنَّكُمْ

دَخَلْنَا ـ خَرَجْتُمْ ـ حَرِيقٌ ـ خُبْزٍ ـ خُبْزًا ـ ذٰلِكَ

هٰذِهِ ـ أَخْبَرَ ـ حِمَارٌ ـ حِمَارًا ـ خَرَجْنَا ـ أَخْرَجَ

---

(30) The letter خ (kh) is the same as the **ch** in Scottish words, such as **loch**. But more from the throat.

(31) In some words the long vowel **ā** (اَ) is expressed by a short vertical stroke over the consonant. For example: هٰذَا (hádhā); ذٰلِكَ (dhālika) etc.

Eleventh Lesson

A

Plural		Singular	
"we"	نَحْنُ	"I"	أَنَا
"you (masc.)"	أَنْتُمْ	"thou (masc.)"	أَنْتَ
"you (fem.)"	أَنْتُنَّ	"thou (fem.)"	أَنْتِ
"they (masc.)"	هُمْ	"he"	هُوَ
"they (fem.)"	هُنَّ	"she"	هِيَ

<u>Translate</u>: We and thou (masc.); you (masc.) and they (masc.); he and she; they (fem.) and you (fem.); thou (fem.) and I; we and she; I and he.

B

Plural		Singular	
"we have written" or "we wrote"	كَتَبْنَا	"I have written" or "I wrote"	كَتَبْتُ
"you (m.) have written" or "you wrote"	كَتَبْتُمْ	"thou (m.) hast written" or "thou wrotest"	كَتَبْتَ
"you (f.) have written" or "you wrote"	كَتَبْتُنَّ	"thou (f.) hast written" or "thou wrotest"	كَتَبْتِ
"they (m.) have written" or "they wrote" (32)	كَتَبُوا	"he has written" or "he wrote"	كَتَبَ
"they (f.) have written" or "they wrote"	كَتَبْنَ	"she has written" or "she wrote"	كَتَبْتْ

(32) An ا is written but **not pronounced** after the و ending of some verbal forms e.g. كَتَبُوا , pronounce: katabū.

Translate: We have written; they (masc.) have written; he wrote; we wrote; he has written; you (masc.) have written; thou (fem.) hast written; I wrote; you (fem.) wrote; thou (fem.) wrotest; I have written; you (masc.) wrote; thou (masc.) wrotest

Conjugate as above the following four verbs:

تَرَكْتُ "I have left" or "I left"

كَسَرْتُ "I have broken" or "I broke"

أَكَلْتُ "I have eaten" or "I ate"

قَسَمْتُ "I have divided" or "I divided"

Twelfth Lesson
(read and translate)

١. مَا هٰذَا ؟- هٰذَا حِمَارٌ ٢. هٰذَا حِمَارِي ٣. هٰذَا كَلْبُكَ ٤. حِمَارِي أَكَلَ وَحِمَارُكَ مَا أَكَلَ ٥. أَنَا أَكَلْتُ وَأَنْتَ مَا أَكَلْتَ ٦. مَنْ كَتَبَ وَمَنْ رَسَمَ ؟- سَلِيمٌ كَتَبَ وَأَنَا رَسَمْتُ ٧. لِي أَخٌ وَأُخْتٌ وَلَهُ أَخٌ وَأُخْتٌ ٨. شَاكِرٌ أَكْبَرُ مِنْ أَخِي ٩. لِي جَمَلٌ وَلَكَ جَمَلٌ. جَمَلُكَ أَكْبَرُ وَأَسْمَنُ مِنْ جَمَلِي ١٠ مَنْ خَرَجَ مِنْ بُسْتَانِي ؟- أَخِي خَرَجَ مِنْ هُنَاكَ

11. مَنْ أَكَلَ فِي بُسْتَانِي؟ – أَبِي أَكَلَ هُنَاكَ 12. أَخِي

كَتَبَ هُنَا وَأُخْتِي كَتَبَتْ هُنَاكَ 13. جَمَلِي أَكَلَ

هُنَا وَجَمَلُكَ أَكَلَ هُنَاكَ 14. هُمْ كَتَبُوا وَمَا رَسَمُوا

15. هُنَّ رَسَمْنَ وَمَا كَتَبْنَ 16. نَحْنُ خَرَجْنَا مِنْ

بُسْتَانِي وَأَنْتُمْ خَرَجْتُمْ مِنْ هُنَاكَ 17. هُمْ رَسَمُوا

وَأَنْتُنَّ مَا رَسَمْتُنَّ 18. نَحْنُ وَأَنْتُمْ. هُمْ وَأَنْتُنَّ.

أَنَا وَهُنَّ. أَنْتَ وَهُوَ. هِيَ وَأَنْتِ 19. كَتَبْنَا

وَمَا رَسَمْنَا. رَسَمْتُمْ وَمَا كَتَبْتُمْ. كَتَبُوا وَمَا رَسَمُوا.

Vocabulary: 30. مَا "what?" 31. هَذَا "this" 32. حِمَارٌ

"ass" (هَذَا حِمَارِي "this is my ass", هَذَا حِمَارٌ "this is an ass")

33. كَتَبَ "to write" 34. مَا "not" 35. مَنْ "who?" 36. أَكَلَ "to eat"

37. رَسَمَ "to sketch", "to draw" 38. أَخٌ "brother"

39. أُخْتٌ "sister" 40. جَمَلٌ "camel" 41. خَرَجَ "to go out" 42. هُنَاكَ

"there" 43. هُنَا "here" 44—50 نَحْنُ هُنَّ هُمْ etc. See above p. 25.

Note 1: The Arabic verb usually has three radical letters

as كَتَبَ. أَكَلَ. رَسَمَ.

Note 2: In dictionaries the Arabic verb is found in its

3rd pers. sing. masc. active form. This form is generally given in the dictionaries as the infinitive of the verb. Thus we say:

أَكَلَ "to eat" ; كَتَبَ "to write", although it really means

"he ate" ; "he wrote"

Translate: 1. I ate (have eaten) and thou (fem.) didst not eat   2. They (masc.) wrote (have written) and we drew (have drawn)   3. My father went out of my garden   4. My mother went out of my vineyard   5. We wrote and he did not write   6. My pupil has a brother and a sister and thou (fem.) hast a brother   7. Thy (masc.) camel ate (has eaten) and my ass did not eat   8. What is this ? — this is a camel 9. Your (masc.) dog is bigger and fatter than my dog   10. We ate (have eaten) in my garden   11. He ate (has eaten) and she did not eat   12. My sister wrote (has written) and you (fem.) did not write   13. Your (masc.) brother went out of my vineyard   14. We ate and she did not eat.

Thirteenth Lesson

(33) (t) ة

مَدِينَةٌ (madinatun) سَنَةٌ (sánatun) لَهُ (láhu)

سَيَّارَةٌ (sayyáratun) كَبِيرَةٌ (kabíratun) بِهِ

---

(33) The letter ه with two points above it (ة) is pronounced like

ت (t). For example سَنَةٌ (sánatun).

The letter ة (t) is found only at the end of the words (nouns or adjectives).

The letter ة is called in Arabic **Tā Marbúta** and the letter

ت is called **Tā Tawíla.**

بَقَرَةٌ (báqaratun) بَقَرَةٍ (báqaratin) أَنْ

آمَالٌ ('ámalun) (34) آكِلٌ ('ákilun) أَنْ ('an)

آمُرُ ('ámuru) آخُذُ ('akhudhu)

هِرَّةٌ آمِرُ هِرَّةٍ سَمِينَةٌ سَنَةٍ

يَبْدَأُ — سَنَةٌ — بُسْتَانًا — سَيَّارَةٌ — سَيَّارَتِي — كَتَبَهُ

يَقْرَءَانِ — قَرَآ — آمُرُ — رَآهُ .

---

(34) Whenever ء is written above an **alif** and is followed by ا

(thus : اأَ) or by a vowelless **Alif** (thus : اأ), then the **Hamza** and its vowel are dropped and one **Alif** only is written, while above it is put the sign ‾ called **Mádda**, which is pronounced 'ā e.g. آكُلُ ('ākulu) instead of أَأْكُلُ. قُرْآنٌ (qur'ānun) instead of قُرْأَانٌ .

Note: The ء in words like سُؤَالٌ (su'ālun) and يَبْتَدِئَانِ (yabtadi'āni) is not changed into آ because the ء in both cases is not above **Alif** (ا) .

ط (t) (35) طَطَطُ (titatu)

(36)(hírratan)هِرَّةٌ(táhana)طَحَنَ(tíbbun)طَبُّ

طِفْلٌ (latífun) لَطِيفٌ (báqaratan) بَقَرَةٌ

(tálaba) طَلَبَ (yátlubu) يَطْلُبُ (tíflun)

طَهَّرَ ــ نَطْلُبُ ــ طَلَبْنَا ــ لَطِيفَةٌ ــ سَقَطَتْ

مَكْتُوبَةً ــ سَمِينَةً ــ بَكَيْتَ ــ رَبُّهُ ــ وَسِيلَةً .

ظ (z) (37)

(mátarun) مَطَرٌ (názara) نَظَرَ (nazífun) نَظِيفٌ

مَا (madínatan) مَدِينَةٌ (tabíbun) طَبِيبٌ

---

(35) The letter ط is an emphatic **t** sound produced by the tongue being set against the palate instead of the teeth.

The letter ط will be designated in the English transcription by **t**.

(36) The **Tauwin** over the letter ة is not followed by an **Alif** (see above page 17 (24)). For example سَنَةً (sánatan).

(37) The letter ظ is an emphatic **z** sound produced by the tongue being set against the palate instead of the teeth.

The letter ظ will be designated in the English transcription by **z**.

يَنْظُرُ (yánzuru) ظَنَنْتُ (zanántu) يَظِلُّ

(yuzíllu) نَظَرْنَا (nazárna) لَفَظَ (láfaza)

ظَنَّ نَظَرَ ظِلَّ مُظِلٌّ مَلْفُوظٌ

ظُهْرٌ مُطَهَّرٌ لَفْظٌ مَطْلُوبٌ طَارَ

رَبَطَ مَرْبُوطَةٌ جَرِيدَةً آخُذُ

قُرْآنٌ أَنْبَأَ تُنْبِئَانِ رَبَّةٌ رَبَّةٍ رَبَّةً

مَرْحَبَةٌ رَحْمَةً حِكْمَةً مَدِينَةٌ مَدِينَةً

ظُنُونٌ ـ قَرَأَ ـ قَرَآ ـ مَبْسُوطٌ ـ تَرَكَ ـ طَرِيقَةٌ

طُرُقٌ ـ نَظَرْنَا ـ خَمْسَةٌ ـ خَمْسَةٍ ـ خَمْسَةً ـ آكِلٌ

رَبَطَتْ ـ آكِلَةٌ ـ يَقْرَآنِ ـ حَرَكَةٌ ـ حَرَكَةٌ

ظَهَرَتْ ـ ظَاهِرٌ ـ لَفَظَتْ ـ يَظِنُّ ـ ظَنَنْتَ ـ شَدِيدٌ

هٰذَا ـ لٰكِنَّ ـ فِكْرَةٍ ـ فِكْرَةً ـ كَلْبًا ـ حِمَارًا

أَرْنَبًا ـ مَدِينَةً.

Fourteenth Lesson
(read and translate)

خَيْمَةٌ (kháymatun) "tent".

خَيْمَتِي (kháymati) "my tent" خَيْمَتُكَ (kháymatuka)

"thy (masc.) tent" خَيْمَتُكِ (kháymatuki) "thy (fem.) tent" خَيْمَتُهُ

(kháymatuhu) "his tent" خَيْمَتُهَا (kháymatuhā) "her tent" خَيْمَتُنَا

(kháymatunā) "our tent" خَيْمَتُكُمْ (kháymatukum) "your (masc.)

tent" خَيْمَتُكُنَّ (khaymatukúnna) "your (masc.) tent" خَيْمَتُهُمْ

(kháymatuhum) "their (masc.) tent" خَيْمَتُهُنَّ (khaymatuhúnna)

"their (fem.) tent".

Plural		Singular	
"our tent"	خَيْمَتُنَا	"my tent"	خَيْمَتِي
"your (masc.) tent"	خَيْمَتُكُمْ	"thy (masc.) tent"	خَيْمَتُكَ
"your (fem.) tent"	خَيْمَتُكُنَّ	"thy (fem.) tent"	خَيْمَتُكِ
"their (masc.) tent"	خَيْمَتُهُمْ	"his tent"	خَيْمَتُهُ
"their (fem.) tent"	خَيْمَتُهُنَّ	"her tent"	خَيْمَتُهَا

Note : Nouns ending in ة (Tā Marbuta) change the ة

into ت (Tā Ṭawila), when the Possessive Pronouns are attached

to them. For example خَيْمَةٌ "tent"; خَيْمَتِي "my tent"; خَيْمَتُكَ

"thy (masc.) tent" etc.

<u>Translate</u>: "our tent"; "thy (masc.) tent"; "his tent"; "your (fem.) tent"; "their (masc.) tent"; "thy (fem.) tent"; "my tent"; "her tent"; "your (masc.) tent"; "their (fem.) tent".

Declinate the following two nouns :

"cow" بَقَرَةٌ   "newspaper" جَرِيدَةٌ

"my cow" بَقَرَتِي   "my newspaper" جَرِيدَتِي

"thy (masc.) cow" بَقَرَتُكَ   "thy (masc.) newspaper" جَرِيدَتُكَ

etc.   etc.

and also :

"hare" أَرْنَبٌ   "butter" زُبْدَةٌ   "town"; "city" مَدِينَةٌ

"camel" جَمَلٌ   "pupil" تِلْمِيذٌ   "tribe" قَبِيلَةٌ   "jar" جَرَّةٌ

(read and translate)

١. كَرْمِي بَعِيدٌ وَكَرْمُكَ قَرِيبٌ مِنْ هُنَا ٢. بَيْتُهُ
قَرِيبٌ مِنْ هُنَا وَبُسْتَانُهُ بَعِيدٌ مِنْ هُنَا ٣. مَنْ قَرَأَ
وَمَنْ كَتَبَ؟ – أُخْتِي قَرَأَتْ وَأَنَا كَتَبْتُ ٤. مَا قَرَأَتْ
أُخْتُكَ؟ – أُخْتِي قَرَأَتْ فِي كِتَابِي ٥. كَلْبِي أَسْوَدُ
وَكَلْبُكَ أَحْمَرُ ٦. لِي حِبْرٌ أَزْرَقُ وَلَكَ حِبْرٌ أَسْوَدُ
٧. دَفْتَرِي ثَقِيلٌ وَدَفْتَرُكَ خَفِيفٌ ٨. أَخِي قَرَأَ فِي
جَرِيدَتِي وَجَارِي كَتَبَ فِي دَفْتَرِي ٩. هُنَّ قَرَأْنَ

وَهُمْ كَتَبُوا .10 نَحْنُ كَتَبْنَا وَأَنْتُمْ قَرَأْتُمْ .11 بُسْتَانِي

بَعِيدٌ مِنْ هُنَا وَبُسْتَانُكَ أَبْعَدُ مِنْهُ .12 كَرْمِي قَرِيبٌ

مِنْ هُنَا وَكَرْمُهُ أَبْعَدُ مِنْهُ .13 حِبْرِي أَزْرَقُ وَحِبْرُكَ

أَسْوَدُ .14 دِيكِي ثَقِيلٌ وَدِيكُهُ خَفِيفٌ .15 هُوَ

قَرَأَ فِي جَرِيدَتِي وَهِيَ مَا قَرَأَتْ.

Vocabulary: 51. بَعِيدٌ "far" (أَبْعَدُ مِنْ "farther than")

52. قَرِيبٌ "near" (أَقْرَبُ مِنْ "nearer than") 53. قَرَأَ "to read"

(See above page 30 Notes 1-2) 54. أَسْوَدُ "black" 55. أَحْمَرُ "red"

56. أَزْرَقُ "blue" 57. حِبْرٌ "ink" 58. ثَقِيلٌ "heavy" (أَثْقَلُ مِنْ

"heavier than") 59. خَفِيفٌ "light (in weight)" 60. جَرِيدَةٌ

"newspaper" 61. جَارٌ "neighbour".

Note : مِنْ "from"; "of"; "than".

مِنِّي "from (of) me"; "than I"; مِنْكَ "from (of) thee (masc.)";

مِنْكِ "from (of) thee (fem.)"; مِنْهُ ، مِنْهَا ، مِنَّا (instead of

etc. مِنْكُمْ ، مِنْكُنَّ).

Translate: 1. Thy (masc) sister wrote and I read

2. Where is thy (fem.) neighbour ? — he is in my vineyard

3. Her ink is black and his ink is blue   4. Their (fem.) garden
is nearer than my vineyard   5. Thy (masc.) cock is heavier
than my cock   6. What did he read ? — he read my
newspaper   7. Your house is nearer than my house
8. I read and you (masc.) wrote   9. I wrote and my neighbour
read   10. We read and they (masc.) did not read   11. She
wrote and her sister did not write   12. She ate and he
did not eat   13. His house is bigger than my huose   14. His
copy-book is heavier than my copy-book   15. Where is
your (masc.) dog ? — my dog is in my garden.

Fifteenth Lesson

Conjugate the following two verbs :

•I entered• دَخَلْتُ   "I drank" شَرِبْتُ

"thou (masc.) enteredst" دَخَلْتَ   •thou (masc.) drankest• شَرِبْتَ

"thou (fem.) enteredst• دَخَلْتِ   "thou (fem.) drankest" شَرِبْتِ

•he entered• دَخَلَ   "he drank" شَرِبَ

etc.   etc.

and also :

•to فَهِمَ   "to ride" رَكِبَ (See above page 30 notes 1-2) ;

understand• ; فَتَحَ "to open".

(read and translate)

١. مَنْ شَرِبَ وَمَنْ أَكَلَ؟ – أَخِي شَرِبَ وَأَنَا
أَكَلْتُ ٢. هُمْ أَكَلُوا وَمَا شَرِبُوا وَهُنَّ شَرِبْنَ
وَمَا أَكَلْنَ ٣. أَرْنَبِي شَرِبَ وَأَرْنَبُكَ مَا شَرِبَ

4. أَرْنَبُهُ أَسْمَنُ مِنْ أَرْنَبِي ‏، 5. أَخِي دَخَلَ كَرْمِي
وَجَارُكَ خَرَجَ مِنْهُ ‏، 6. لِي خَرُوفٌ سَمِينٌ وَلَهَا
خَرُوفٌ سَمِينٌ ‏، 7. خَرُوفُهُ كَبِيرٌ وَخَرُوفِي أَكْبَرُ
مِنْهُ ‏، 8. أَنْتَ أَكْبَرُ مِنْ أَخِي وَأَنَا أَكْبَرُ مِنْكَ
9. تِلْمِيذُكَ كَبِيرٌ وَتِلْمِيذُهَا أَكْبَرُ مِنْهُ ‏، 10. مَنْ خَرَجَ
مِنْ بُسْتَانِي ؟ – جَدِّي خَرَجَ مِنْهُ ‏، 11. جَدَّتِي دَخَلَتْ
بُسْتَانِي وَخَرَجَتْ مِنْهُ ‏، 12. أَيْنَ جَدُّكَ وَجَدَّتُكَ ؟
– جَدِّي وَجَدَّتِي فِي كَرْمِي ‏، 13. أَبِي وَجَدِّي فِي
بُسْتَانِي وَأُمِّي وَجَدَّتِي فِي كَرْمِي .

Vocabulary: 62. شَرِبَ "to drink" (See above page 30

notes 1-2) 63 دَخَلَ "to enter" 64. خَرُوفٌ lamb. 65. جَدٌّ

"grand-father" 66. جَدَّةٌ "grand-mother" .

Translate: 1. Thy (masc.) grand-father has written and
my father has read   2. Your (masc.) lamb is fatter than
my lamb   3. Where is our mother ? — your (fem.) mother is
in my vineyard   4. Thy (fem.) pupil is big and my pupil
is bigger than he   5. His grand-mother entered my
garden   6. My camel drank and her camel did ont drink
7. They (masc.) drank and we did not drink   8. He went out
of my house   9. My house is nearer than his house   10. My
sister drank and his sister did not drink   11. Her elephant is
bigger than my elephant.

Sixteenth Lesson

(38) ص (s) صُصَصِ (sisusa)

صَيدٌ (sáydun) يَصُومُ (yasùmu) صَامَ (sáma)

فِي (fi) أُكْتُبْ ('uktub) صَدِيقٍ (sadiqin)

(39) فِي أَلْبَيْتِ (qála-k-tub) قَالَ اُكْتُبْ

('albáytu-l-kabíru) أَلْبَيْتُ أَلْكَبِيرُ (fi-l-báyti)

---

(38) The letter ص is an emphatic **s** sound produced by the tongue being set against the palate instead of the teeth,

The letter ص will be designated in the English transcription by **ṣ**.

(39) The Arabic word never begins with a vowelless letter, therefore in cases in which the word should begin with a vowelless letter, a **Hamza** with **Alif** are attached to the beginning of it.

For example: إِرْكَبْ ؛ (أُكْتُبْ ؛ كْتُبْ) "write!" (instead of أُكْتُبْ ؛ كْتُبْ)

"ride!" (instead of رْكَبْ).

This **Hamza** with its vowel are pronounced only when the word is at the begining of a sentence. But in the middle of it the **Hamza** with its vowel are dropped and the sign ◡ called **Wasla** is put over the **Alif** in place of the **Hamza**. In this case the **Alif** is not pronounced and only serves to conbine the following vowelless letter with the last vowel of the preceding word, and then the two words are read as **if they were one.** For example قَالَ اُكْتُبْ pronounce:

أَلْكَرْمُ الْكَبِيرُ ('alkármu-l-kabíru) (min) مِنْ

صَارَ (sára) (mína-l-báyti) مِنَ الْبَيْتِ

---

qála-k-túb •he said: write!•; قَالَ لَهُ أَرْكَبْ pronounce:

qála láhu-r-káb •he said to him: ride!•.

The **Hamza** which is changed in the middle of a sentence in the above-mentioned way into **Wasla** is called in Arabic **Hamzat-l-wasl.**

Note : If the word preceding a **Wasla** ends with a vowelless consonant, then a vowel (generally i) is given to this final consonant. For example قَالَتِ اشْرَبْ (qálalati-sh-ráb)

•she said : drink !• (قَالَتْ •she said•).

In the preposition مِنْ •from• the final ن receives the vowel **a** before the **Wasla** of the Article (see below page 57). For example مِنَ الْبُسْتَانِ (mina-l-bustáni) •from the garden•.

In other cases it receives the usual **i**. For example مِنِ ابْنِكَ (míni-b-níka) •from thy (masc.) son•.

In the Suffixes تُمْ ، كُمْ ، هُمْ the final م receives the vowel **u** before the **Wasla**. For example بَيْتُهُمُ الْجَدِيدُ

báytuhumu-l-gadídu) •their (masc.) new house• (بَيْتُهُمْ •their

masc.) house•; بَيْتُكُمُ الْجَدِيدُ •your (masc.) new house•

•your (masc.) house•; رَأَيْتُمُ الْبَيْتَ •you (masc.) بَيْتُكُمْ

aw the house• (رَأَيْتُمْ •you (masc.) saw•).

أَنَا رَأَيْتُ ٱلْكَلْبَ فِي ٱلْبُسْتَانِ.

رَصِيفٌ ــ صَاحِبٌ ــ أَصْحَابٌ ــ صَاحِبُ ٱلْبَيْتِ

بَيْتٌ ــ ٱلْبَيْتُ ٱلْجَدِيدُ ــ ٱلْبَيْتُ ٱلْقَدِيمُ ــ ٱلْكَبِيرُ

صَارَ ــ صَارَتْ ــ صَدِيقٌ ــ يَصُومُ ٱلْوَلَدُ.

ض (d) (40)

أَرْضٌ (ʼárdun) ضَرَبَ (dáraba) مَضْرُوب

(madrúbun) ضَحِكَ (dáhika) أَضَرَّ (ʼadárra)

مَرِيضٌ (maridun) رَدَّ (rádda) فَرْضٌ (fárdun)

قُرُودٌ (qurúdun) قُرُوضٌ (qurúdun)

فَرْدٌ ضَرَبْتَ دَرَسَتْ أَرْضِي

يَضْرِبُ ــ قَبَضَ ــ أَضَرَّ ــ مَضَيْتَ ــ مَدَّ ــ يَضُرُّ

دِيكٌ ــ دُيُوكٌ ــ ضَحِكَ ــ يَضْحَكُ ــ مَرَضَ.

---

(40) The letter ض is an emphatic **d** sound produced by the tongue being set against the palate instead of the teeth. The letter ض will be designated in the English transcription by **d**.

لا (lā)(٤١)

لِأُمِّي (li'ummī) أَلْأَبُ (al'ábu) لِأَبِي (li'ábī) لَأُمِّي

أَلْإِسْلَامُ (al'islámu) إِلَّا ('íllā) لَأَنَّ (li'ánna) لِأَنَّ ('illā)

لَابِسٌ (lábisun) لَا (lā) أَلَّا ('állā)

أَلْإِرْشَادُ أَلْأَرْنَبُ أَلْأَسِيرُ لِأَنَّكَ

أَلْأَنْفُ ـ لِأَنِّي ـ إِسْلَامٌ ـ أَلْأُمُّ ـ مَدْرَسَةٌ

بَقَرَتِي ـ لِأَبِي ـ لِأَنَّهُ ـ كَبِيرَةً ـ سَمِينَةً ـ شَرِبَتْ

شَرِبَتِ الْبَقَرَةُ ـ لِأَخِي الْكَبِيرِ ـ لِأُمِّي ـ الْأَخُ

طُرُقٌ ـ صَرَفَ ـ ضَرَبْنَا ـ يَضْرِبُونَ ـ ضَرَرٌ ـ يَظْلِمُ

أَظْلَمَ ـ طَلَبْنَا ـ يَطْلُبُونَ ـ رَبَطْنَا ـ سَقَطَ ـ يُحَرِّكُ

يَظُنُّ ـ شَدِيدَةٌ ـ يَضْحَكُونَ ـ مَضْرُوبٌ ـ صُومِي

---

(٤١) When the letter ل (l) is followed by the letter ا (Alif)

then they are written thus لا. For example لِأَبِي (li'ábī),

لِأُمِّي (li'ummī), لَا (lā).

Seventeenth Lesson

"he has found (he found) me"	وَجَدَنِي
"he has found (he found) thee (masc.)"	وَجَدَكَ
"he has found (he found) thee (fem)."	وَجَدَكِ
" " " " " him (or : it)	وَجَدَهُ
" " " " " her (or : it)	وَجَدَهَا
" " " " " us	وَجَدَنَا
" " " " " YOU (masc.)	وَجَدَكُمْ
" " " " " YOU (fem.)	وَجَدَكُنَّ
" " " " " them (masc.)	وَجَدَهُمْ
" " " " " them (fem.)	وَجَدَهُنَّ

When a personal pronoun is the direct object of a verb,
it is attached to the verb. For example:

وَجَدَ "he found" :

_____

وَجَدَنِي "he found me"; وَجَدَكَ "he found thee (masc.)",

وَجَدَهَا "he found her"; وَجَدَكُمْ "he found you",

"he found them (masc.)" وَجَدَهُنَّ "he found them (fem.)".

وَجَدَتْ "she found":

_____

وَجَدَتْنِي "she found me"; وَجَدَتْكَ "she found thee (masc.)";

وَجَدَتْهُ "she found him (or it)"; وَجَدَتْنَا "she found us" etc.

وَجَدْنَا "we found":

_____

وَجَدْنَاكَ "we found him"; وَجَدْنَاهَا "we found her"; وَجَدْنَاهُ

"we found thee (masc.)"; وَجَدْنَاكُمْ "we found you (masc.)" etc.

وَجَدُوا "they (masc.) found":

_____

وَجَدُونِي "they (masc.) found me"; وَجَدُوهُ "they (m.) found

him"; وَجَدُوهَا "they (m.) found her"; وَجَدُوكُمْ "they (masc.)

found you (masc.)" etc.

The personal pronouns in the objective case are the same
as the possessive pronouns (see above page 22 and page 44).

Note 1: The pronominal suffix of the first person in the

objective case is نِي , while the suffix of the

possessive pronoun in the first person is ِي . For

example وَجَدَ ("he found me" (وَجَدَنِي "he

found"); بَيْتِي "my house" (بَيْتٌ "house").

Note 2: The final **Alif** (ا) in the 3rd plur. masc. (see above
page 28 (32)) is dropped before the suffixes. For
example وَجَدُوا "they (masc.) found me" وَجَدُونِي

"they found" (وَجَدُوهُ "they (masc.) found him" etc.

__Note 3:__ The final م (m) in the second person plur. masc. is dropped and in its place a و is put before the pronominal suffixes. For example وَجَدْتُونِي "you (masc.) found me" (وَجَدْتُمْ "you (masc.) found") وَجَدْتُوهُ "you (masc.) found him".

Eighteenth Lesson
(read and translate)

١. أَيْنَ وَجَدَ إِبْرَاهِيمُ حِصَانِي؟ ‎- هُوَ وَجَدَهُ فِي بُسْتَانِي ٢. أَيْنَ وَجَدَ أَحْمَدُ بَقَرَتِي؟ ‎- هُوَ وَجَدَهَا فِي كَرْمِي ٣. مَنْ ضَرَبَ أَخِي؟ ‎- جَارُكَ ضَرَبَهُ ٤. مَنْ وَجَدَكُمْ فِي بُسْتَانِي؟ ‎- جَارُكَ وَجَدَنَا هُنَاكَ ٥. مَنْ ضَرَبَكُمْ؟ ‎- جَارُكَ ضَرَبَنَا ٦. مَنْ أَكَلَ خُبْزِي؟ ‎- نَحْنُ أَكَلْنَاهُ ٧. مَنْ شَرِبَ حَلِيبِي؟ ‎- نَحْنُ شَرِبْنَاهُ ٨. مَنْ ضَرَبَكَ؟ ‎- جَارُكَ ضَرَبَنِي ٩. مَنْ كَسَرَ فِنْجَانِي؟ ‎- أُخْتُكَ كَسَرَتْهُ ١٠. مَنْ ضَرَبَ حِمَارِي؟ ‎- تِلْمِيذُكَ ضَرَبَهُ ١١. أَخِي مَا

كَسَرَ فِنْجَانِي. أُخْتِي كَسَرَتْهُ 12. أُخْتِي شَرِبَتْ

حَلِيبِي وَأَخِي مَا شَرِبَهُ 13. مَنْ ضَرَبَ جَمَلِي ؟—

أَحْمَدُ ضَرَبَهُ 14. حِصَانُكُمْ أَكْبَرُ وَأَثْمَنُ مِنْ حِصَانِي

15. لِي حِبْرٌ أَسْوَدُ وَلَهُ حِبْرٌ أَخْضَرُ 16. لَهَا كَلْبٌ

أَسْوَدُ وَلَكُمْ كَلْبٌ أَبْيَضُ 17. لِي حِصَانٌ وَحِمَارٌ

وَلَكُمْ ثَوْرٌ وَجَمَلٌ 18. فِنْجَانُكَ أَكْبَرُ مِنْ فِنْجَانِي.

Vocabulary: 67 وَجَدَ "to find" (see above page 30. Notes 1-2); 68 إِبْرَاهِيم "Ibrahim" (proper noun masculine); 69 حِصَانٌ "horse"; 70 أَحْمَدُ "Ahmad" (proper noun masculine); 71 بَقَرَةٌ "cow"; 72 ضَرَبَ "to strike" "to beat"; 73 خُبْزٌ "bread" 74. حَلِيبٌ "milk"; 75 كَسَرَ "to break"; 76 فِنْجَانٌ "cup"; 77 أَخْضَرُ "green"; 78 أَبْيَضُ "white".

Translate: 1. Who found my book?— my sister found it   2. Who has beaten my pupil? — Our neighbour has beaten him   3. Who broke my cup?— their (masc.) sister broke it   4. Your (fem.) ink is black and our ink is blue   5. Her ink is green and his ink is red   6. Ibrahim is bigger than my brother   7. Ahmad broke my cup   8. I have an ass and she has an ass. Her ass is fatter than my ass   9. His horse is big and thy (masc.) horse is bigger than it   11. Your (masc.) dog is black and their (fem.) dog is white   12. Her brother has beaten my ox   13. Where did he find my cup? — he found it in my vineyard   14. We found her. She found him I found her. Thou (masc.) hast found me.

Nineteenth Lesson

"I shall write", or "I write"	أَكْتُبُ
"thou (masc.) wilt write", or "thou writest"	تَكْتُبُ
"thou (fem.) wilt write", or "thou writest"	تَكْتُبِينَ
"he will write", or "he writes"	يَكْتُبُ
"she will write", or "she writes"	تَكْتُبُ
"we shall write", or "we write"	نَكْتُبُ
"you (masc.) will write", or "you write"	تَكْتُبُونَ
"you (fem.) will write", or "you write"	تَكْتُبْنَ
"they (masc.) will write", or "they write"	يَكْتُبُونَ
"they (fem.) will write", or "they write"	يَكْتُبْنَ

The Arabic verb has two main tenses which, however, are not real tenses in their European sense. These two main tenses are generally known as Perfect and Imperfect.

The Perfect denotes a finished action, most often referring to the **past**, and the Imperfect denotes an unfinished action, most often referring to the **present** or **future**.

<u>Translate:</u> He will write ; we shall write ; They (masc.) will write ; he wrote (See above page 28) ; I have written ; he has written ; I wrote ; he writes ; she will write ; we write ; she writes ;

we have written; they (masc.) have written; thou (masc.) wilt write; you (masc.) will write; I shall write; they (fem.) wrote; we write; you (fem.) have written; she wrote; they (fem.) will write; I write; they (masc.) write.

The vowel of the second radical letter (see above page 30, note 1) of the Imperfect can be **u**, **a** or **i**. For example يَكْتُبُ (yáktubu) "he will write" or "he writes"; يَشْرَبُ (yáshrabu) "he will drink" or "he drinks"; يَضْرِبُ (yádribu) "he will beat" or "he beats".

Conjugate as above the two following verbs :

"I shall beat" ("I beat") أَضْرِبُ	"I shall drink" ("I drink") أَشْرَبُ
تَضْرِبُ	تَشْرَبُ
تَضْرِبِينَ	تَشْرَبِينَ
يَضْرِبُ	يَشْرَبُ
etc.	etc.

<u>and also</u> : أَرْكَبُ "I shall ride" or "I ride"; أَفْهَمُ "I shall understand" or "I understand"; أَنْزِلُ "I shall descend" or, "I descend"; أَخْرُجُ "I shall go out" or "I go out".

<u>Translate:</u> he will drink; we beat; they (masc.) beat; I drink; you (masc.) will beat; she will drink; thou (fem.) wilt drink"; they (fem.) will beat : we shall drink; thou (masc.) wilt beat; you (fem.) drink; we beat; I shall drink.

Twentieth Lesson
(read and translate)

١. مَنْ يَكْتُبُ وَمَنْ يَرْسُمُ ؟– أَيِّي تَكْتُبُ
وَأَخْتِي تَرْسُمُ   ٢. كُمْ كَتَبُوا وَأَنْتُمْ مَا كَتَبْتُمْ ٣. هُمْ
يَكْتُبُونَ وَأَنْتُمْ لَا تَكْتُبُونَ   ٤. هُنَّ شَرِبْنَ وَأَنْتُنَّ
مَا شَرِبْتُنَّ   ٥. هُنَّ يَشْرَبْنَ وَأَنْتُنَّ لَا تَشْرَبْنَ
٦. بَقَرَتِي تَشْرَبُ الْآنَ وَبَقَرَتُكَ لَا تَشْرَبُ ٧. أَيْنَ
تَكْتُبُ فَاطِمَةُ ؟– هِيَ تَكْتُبُ فِي دَفْتَرِي ٨. صَالِحٌ
كَتَبَ الْآنَ وَأَنَا مَا كَتَبْتُ   ٩. أَيْنَ تَرَكْتَ
ثَوْرِي ؟– تَرَكْتُهُ فِي بُسْتَانِي ١٠. شَاكِرٌ تَرَكَ كِتَابِي
فِي مَدْرَسَتِي   ١١. مَنْ فَتَحَ كِتَابِي ؟– تِلْمِيذِي فَتَحَهُ
١٢. لِي مَائِدَةٌ وَكُرْسِيٌّ وَلَكَ مَائِدَةٌ وَبَنْكٌ
١٣. مَائِدَتُكَ أَكْبَرُ مِنْ مَائِدَتِي ١٤. أَيْنَ أَخِي أَحْمَدُ ؟–
هُوَ فِي مَدْرَسَتِي   ١٥. أُخْتِي فَاطِمَةُ أَكْبَرُ مِنِّي وَأَنَا
أَكْبَرُ مِنْكِ ١٨. مَنْ فَتَحَ كِتَابِي ؟– أَنَا مَا فَتَحْتُهُ.
فَتَحَهُ تِلْمِيذُكَ شَاكِرٌ   ١٩. هِيَ تَخْرُجُ وَأَنْتِ لَا

تَحْرُجِينَ 20. أَنْتَ تَرْسُمُ وَهُوَ لَا يَرْسُمُ 21. إِبْرَهِيمُ
يَكْتُبُ وَفَاطِمَةُ لَا تَكْتُبُ 22. أَنْتُمْ خَرَجْتُمْ مِنْ
بُسْتَانِي وَهُمْ لَا يَخْرُجُونَ مِنْهُ.

<u>Vocabulary:</u> 79. لَا "not" (particle of negation before the Imperfect)

80. أَلْآنَ "now", "at present" (Note : تَشْرَبُ الْآنَ pronounce:

táshrabu-l-'āna. See above page 40 (39) and page 32 (34)) 81. فَاطِمَةُ

"Fāṭima" (proper noun, feminine) 82. صَالِحٌ "Ṣāliḥ" (proper noun, masc.)

83. تَرَكَ "to leave" (Imperfect: أَتْرُكُ) 84. مَدْرَسَةٌ "school"

85. فَتَحَ "to open" (Imperfect: أَفْتَحُ) 86. مَائِدَةٌ "table"

87. كُرْسِيٌّ "chair" 88. بَنْكٌ "bench".

<u>Translate</u>: 1. Thy (masc.) brother wrote and we did not write   2. We shall write and you (masc.) will not write   3. Thy (masc.) table is bigger than my table   4. I have a chair and a bench and she has a table and a chair   5. Where did Salim write ? — he wrote in my vineyard   6. His ox is black and her ox is white   7. Your pupil broke my chair   8. Thy (fem.) horse is bigger and fatter than my horse   9. Where is her brother ?— he is in my school   10. They (masc.) will write and he will not write   11. Our sister drank and thy sister did not drink   12. Where is his lamb?— his lamb is in my garden   13. I have written and my grand-father did not write   14. Your (fem.) house is nearer than my house   15. We have an ox and an ass and he has a camel and a cow   16. She has a sister and I have a sister and a brother.

Twenty-first Lesson

(42) (‘a’i‘u) عَعِعُ (‘)ع

إِسْمَع (má‘a) مَع (‘árabun) عَرَبٌ (’isma‘)

يَعْلِمُ (sámi‘at) سَمِعَتْ (má‘i) مَعِي (yu‘állimu)

عَلَى (‘álā) رَعَى (rá‘ā) رَأَى (rá’ā) (43)

بَنَى (mátā) مَتَى (bákā) بَكَى (bánā)

---

(42) The letter ع is a very strong guttural produced by the compression of the throat and the expulsion of the breath.

The letter ع will be designated in the English transcription by ‘

(43) At the end of a word the ā is often expressed by ى

(a followed by ى without its two points and without **Sukun**)

For example أَلْقَى (’álqā) "he threw"; بَنَى "he built".

As soon as this ى receives a suffix, it becomes an اَ

For example أَلْقَاهُ "he threw it"; بَنَاهُ "he built it".

ى is called in Arabic **Alif Maqsūra** and also **Alif bisurati-l-Ya**.

سَمِعَ إِلَى رَمَى مَعَكَ خَتَّى

مَعْلُومٌ ـ يُعَلِّمُ ـ عَرَبِيٌّ ـ عَرَبِيَّةٌ ـ مَعْنَا ـ صَنَعَ

صَنَعَتْ ـ صِنَاعَةٌ ـ فَعَلَ ـ عَدَدٌ ـ عَدَّ ـ مُسْتَعِدٌّ

(٩٤) (gh) غ

بَلَغَ (ghّayri) غَيْرِي (مَغْرِبٌ (mّaghribun

(ghّanamun) غَنَمٌ (shّughlun) شُغْلٌ (bّalagha) بَلَغَ

يَغْسِلُ (balّighun) بَلِيغٌ (gharّibun) غَرِيبٌ

(ghanّiyun) غَنِيٌّ (yّaghsilu)

رَغِبَ غَرَبَ غَيْرَ يُغَيِّرُ مَبْلَغٌ

غَيْرُكَ ـ يَبْلُغُ ـ غُرْفَةٌ ـ غَلَبَ ـ مَغْلُوبٌ ـ غَالِبٌ

يُغَيِّرُونَ ـ تَغْيِيرٌ ـ غَنَمُكَ ـ أَشْغَالٌ ـ غَرِقَ ـ يَغْرَقُ.

---

(٩٤) The letter غ has a sound like the gargling pronunciation
between **g** and **r**.

The letter غ will be designated in the English transcription by **gh.**

مُعَلِّمُكَ ـ عَلَى ـ عَلَيْكَ ـ عَلَيْنَا ـ مَعَكُمْ ـ مَعَنَا ـ مُغَيِّرٌ

غَيَّرْنَا ـ فَعَلْتَ ـ غَرَبَتْ ـ غَسَلَتْ ـ يَدْعُونَا ـ دَعَوْتُهُ

يُغْرِي ـ غُرْفَتِي ـ نُغَيِّرُ ـ رَغِبَتْ ـ غَنَمُكَ ـ غَنَمُكُمْ

شُغْلٌ ـ رَعَى ـ رَعَيْتَ ـ رَأَى ـ رَأَيْتَ ـ بَنَى ـ بَنَاهُ ـ رَآهُ

بَكَى ـ بَقِيَ ـ يَبْقَى .

Twenty-second Lesson
(read and translate)

١. إِلَى أَيْنَ تَذْهَبُ يَا أَخِي ؟ ـ أَذْهَبُ إِلَى

مَدْرَسَتِي ٢. أَيْنَ كِتَابُكَ ؟ ـ كِتَابِي عَلَى مَائِدَتِي

٣. أُخْتِي خَرَجَتْ مِنْ غُرْفَتِي وَأَخِي مَا خَرَجَ مِنْ

هُنَاكَ ٤. أَخِي رَجَعَ مِنْ يَافَا وَأَبِي يَرْجِعُ غَدًا مِنْ

هُنَاكَ ٥. مُعَلِّمِي ذَهَبَ مَعَ جَدِّي إِلَى مَدْرَسَتِي

٦. مَنْ خَرَجَ مَعَكَ مِنْ غُرْفَتِي ؟ ـ مُعَلِّمُكَ خَرَجَ

مَعِي مِنْ هُنَاكَ ٧. لِي كَلْبٌ كَبِيرٌ وَلَكَ كَلْبٌ صَغِيرٌ

كَلْبُكَ أَصْغَرُ مِنْ كَلْبِي ٨. أَخِي أَصْغَرُ مِنِّي وَأَنَا

أَصْغَرُ مِنْكَ . ٩. جَارِي فَقِيرٌ جِدًّا وَجَارُكَ غَنِيٌّ جِدًّا

10. جَمَلُكَ أَصْغَرُ مِنْ جَمَلِي وَحِمَارُكَ أَكْبَرُ مِنْ حِمَارِي. 11. أَحْمَدُ فَقِيرٌ جِدًّا وَسَلِيمٌ أَفْقَرُ مِنْهُ. 12. إِبْرَاهِيمُ غَنِيٌّ جِدًّا وَشَاكِرٌ أَغْنَى مِنْهُ.

<u>Vocabulary</u>: 89. إِلَى "to". 90. ذَهَبَ "to go"; "to go away" (Imperfect. أَذْهَبُ) 91. يَا "o !" (particle of address) 92. عَلَى "on"; "upon". 93. غُرْفَة "room"; "chamber". 94. رَجَعَ "to return" (Imperfect. يَرْجِعُ) 95. يَافَا Jaffa. 96. غَدًا "to-morrow". 97. مُعَلِّم "teacher". 98. مَعَ "with" (مَعِي "with me" مَعَكَ "with thee (masc.)" مَعَهُ "with him" etc.) 99. صَغِير "small" (أَصْغَرُ مِنْ "smaller than") 100. فَقِير "poor", "needy" (أَفْقَرُ مِنْ "poorer than") 101. غَنِيٌّ "rich" (أَغْنَى مِنْ "richer than") 102. جِدًّا "very".

<u>Translate</u>: 1. Where is my newspaper ? — Thy (masc.) newspaper is on my table   2. His horse is smaller than my horse   3. Her ox is very big   4. Ibrāhīm is richer than my neighbour   5. His neighbour is rich and our neighbour is poor   6. O Salim, where is my book ? — thy book is in my room   7. Your (masc.) garden is smaller than my garden. My garden is very big   8. Thou (masc.) art bigger than my brother   9. Where is my grand-father ? — he is in my room   10. Your (masc.) grand-father is richer than my grand-father.

The order of the Arabic alphabet is as follows:

The letters	Names of the letters	Pronunciation of the letters	The letters	Names of the letters	Pronunciation of the letters
١	'Alif	See page 10 (19); page 19 (26); p. 32 (34); p. 40 (39)	ض	Dād	d. See page 42 (40)
ب	Bā	b.	ط	Tā	t. See page 33 (35)
ت	Tā	t.	ظ	Zā	z. See page 33 (37)
ث	Thā	th. See page 2 (8)	ع	'Ain	See page 52 (42)
ج	Ğim	ğ. See page 25 (28)	غ	Ghain	gh. See p. 53 (44)
ح	Hā	h. See page 26 (29)	ف	Fā	f.
خ	Khā	kh. See p. 27 (30)	ق	Qāf	q. See page 25 (27)
د	Dal	d.	ك	Kāf	k.
ذ	Dhal	dh. See p. 18 (25)	ل	Lām	l.
ر	Rā	r. See page 6 (13)	م	Mim	m.
ز	Zai	z.	ن	Nūn	n.
س	Sin	s.	ه	Hā	h.
ش	Shin	sh.	و	Wāw	w. See page 8 (16)
ص	Sād	s. See page 40 (38)	ي	Yā	y. See page 9 (18)

Twenty-third Lesson

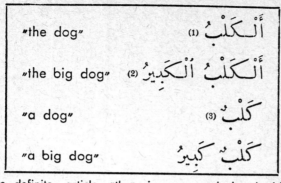

"the dog"	(1) أَلْـكَلْبُ
"the big dog"	(2) أَلْـكَلْبُ الْـكَبِيرُ
"a dog"	(3) كَلْبٌ
"a big dog"	كَلْبٌ كَبِيرٌ

(1) The definite article "the" is expressed in Arabic by the syllable أَلْ, which is prefixed to the nouns and the adjectives. For example أَلْـكَلْبُ "the dog"; أَلْـكَبِيرُ "the big" "the great".

(2) The **Hamza** (see above page 19 (26)) of the article أَلْ is **Hamzat-l-wasl** (see above page 40 (29)). This **Hamza** is therefore pronounced only at the beginning of a sentence. But in the middle of the sentence it becomes a **Wasla** (see above page 40 (39)), which combines the vowelless لْ of the article with the last vowel of the preceding word and the two words are read as if they were one (see above page 40 (39)). For example أَلْبَيْتُ الْـكَبِيرُ, pronounce : albáytu-l-kabĭru "the big house" (الْـكَبِيرُ "the big") ; أَ كَلَ الْـكَلْبُ pronounce: ákala-l-kálbu "the dog ate".

(3) The indefinite article **a (an)** is expresssed in Arabic by the **Tanwin** (see above page 4 (11)). For example كَلْبٌ "a dog;

Note 1: When the noun is qualified by an adjective, the adjective follows it e. g. بَيْتٌ كَبِيرٌ (báytun kabírun) "a big house" **and not**: كَبِيرٌ بَيْتٌ (kabírun báytun) .

If the noun is definite, the adjective also must be made definite by the addition of the article أَلْ thus :

أَلْبَيْتُ الْكَبِيرُ "the big house".

The copula "is" or "are" is not expressed in Arabic e. g. أَلْبَيْتُ كَبِيرٌ "the house is big"; أَلْخَبَّازُ فَقِيرٌ "the baker is poor".

Note 2: هٰذَا كَلْبٌ "this is a dog"; هٰذَا كَلْبٌ كَبِيرٌ "this is a big dog"

هٰذَا الْكَلْبُ "this dog"; هٰذَا الْكَلْبُ الْكَبِيرُ "this big dog"

هٰذَا الْكَلْبُ كَبِيرٌ "this dog is big"

Translate: A big elephant; the big elephant; this elephant; this big elephant; the elephant is big; this elephant is big; the hare is fat; the vineyard is large; the house is small; this house is small; the neighbour is poor; the book is big; a big book; this book is big; the big book; this camel is big and fat; a big ass; an ass; the ass is big and fat; the big horse; this horse is fat; this big horse; a fat cock; a big and fat lamb; this lamb is bigger than my lamb; this bread is cheap; this cup is cheap; the cup is cheap; this camel is fatter than my camel, this house is cheaper than my nouse.

Twenty-fourth Lesson

۱. هٰذَا الْجَمَلُ صَغِيرٌ. هُوَ أَصْغَرُ مِنْ جَمَلِي

۲. هٰذَا الْحِمَارُ رَخِيصٌ وَذٰلِكَ الْحِمَارُ أَرْخَصُ مِنْهُ

۳. ذٰلِكَ الْخَيَّاطُ فَقِيرٌ. هُوَ أَفْقَرُ مِنْ جَارِي ۴. مَنْ
كَانَ الْيَوْمَ فِي غُرْفَتِي ؟ـ زَيْدٌ كَانَ هُنَاكَ وَالْخَبَّازُ
أَيْضًا كَانَ هُنَاكَ ۵. الْحَلَّاقُ كَانَ الْيَوْمَ فِي يَافَا
وَالْحَدَّادُ أَيْضًا كَانَ هُنَاكَ ۶. أُخْتُكَ كَانَتْ فِي بُسْتَانِي
وَفَاطِمَةُ أَيْضًا كَانَتْ هُنَاكَ ۷. أُمِّي كَانَتِ الْيَوْمَ فِي
يَافَا وَأُخْتِي أَيْضًا كَانَتْ هُنَاكَ ۸. أَيْنَ الْكِتَابُ
الْجَدِيدُ ؟ـ الْكِتَابُ الْجَدِيدُ عَلَى مَائِدَتِي فِي غُرْفَتِي
۹. مَتَى رَجَعَ زَيْدٌ مِنْ يَافَا وَمَتَى رَجَعَ الْحَلَّاقُ ؟ـ
زَيْدٌ رَجَعَ مِنْ يَافَا الْيَوْمَ وَالْحَلَّاقُ أَيْضًا رَجَعَ
الْيَوْمَ ۱۰. مَا هٰذَا ؟ـ هٰذَا كَلْبٌ ۱۱. هٰذَا الْكَلْبُ
أَكْبَرُ وَأَثْمَنُ مِنْ كَلْبِي ۱۲. هٰذَا الْبَيْتُ الْجَدِيدُ
أَكْبَرُ مِنْ بَيْتِي وَذٰلِكَ الْبَيْتُ أَصْغَرُ مِنْهُ ۱۳. هٰذَا
الْفِيلُ كَبِيرٌ وَذٰلِكَ الْفِيلُ أَكْبَرُ مِنْهُ ۱۴. مَتَى

رَجَعْتَ مِنْ يَافَا ؟ ـ رَجَعْتُ ٱلْيَوْمَ مِنْ هُنَاكَ

15. جَدُّكَ كَانَ ٱلْيَوْمَ فِي كَرْمِي وَفِي بُسْتَانِي 16. أَيْنَ

ٱلْكَلْبُ ٱلْكَبِيرُ وَأَيْنَ ٱلْحِمَارُ ؟ ـ ٱلْكَلْبُ

ٱلْكَبِيرُ فِي بُسْتَانِي وَٱلْحِمَارُ أَيْضًا فِي بُسْتَانِي.

Vocabulary: 103. ذٰلِكَ "that" 104. رَخِيصٌ "cheap"

105. (ذٰلِكَ ٱلْبَيْتُ "that house") 106. خَيَّاطٌ "tailor" كَانَ

"he was" (كَانَتْ "she was") 107. ٱلْيَوْمَ "to-day" 108. زَيْدٌ

"Zayd" (proper noun, masc.) 109. خَبَّازٌ "baker" 110. أَيْضًا "also" "too"

(أَيْضًا أَنْتَ ؛ أَيْضًا أَخِي and not: أَنْتَ أَيْضًا ؛ أَخِي أَيْضًا)

111. جَدِيدٌ "new" 112. حَدَّادٌ "blacksmith" 113. حَلَّاقٌ "barber"

114. مَتَى "when ?".

Translate: 1. Thy (masc.) book is cheaper than my book
2. This camel is big and that camel is small   3. This tailor is
rich and that baker is poor   4. The barber was in Jaffa and
the blacksmith too was there   5. This new house is bigger
than my house   6. That new book is cheaper than my new
book   7. When did you return from Jaffa ? — I have returned
to-day from there   8. Where is the tailor ? — He is in my room
9. This dog is bigger and fatter than my dog   11. A big
garden. The big garden. This big garden. This garden is big.
That garden. That big garden. That garden is big.

Twenty-fifth Lesson

"a baker visited me"	زَارَنِي خَبَّازٌ (1)
"the baker visited me"	زَارَنِي الْخَبَّازُ
"the house of a baker"	بَيْتُ خَبَّازٍ
"the house of the baker"	بَيْتُ الْخَبَّازِ
"he saw a baker"	هُوَ رَأَى خَبَّازًا
"he saw the baker"	هُوَ رَأَى الْخَبَّازَ
"from the baker"	مِنَ الْخَبَّازِ (2)
"to the baker"	إِلَى الْخَبَّازِ
"on the baker"	عَلَى الْخَبَّازِ

(1) In Arabic there are three cases: Nominative, Genitive and Accusative.

These three cases are expressed as follows:

a) The Nominative is expressed by the **Tanwin** ٌ (un) if the noun is indefinite, and by the vowel ُ (u) if it is definite. Thus:

زَارَنِي خَبَّازٌ "a baker visited me"

زَارَنِي الْخَبَّازُ "the baker visited me"

b) The Genitive is expressed by the **Tanwin** ٍ (in) if the noun is indefinite and by the vowel ِ (i) if it is definite. Thus:

بَيْتُ خَبَّازٍ "the house **of a** baker"

بَيْتُ الْخَبَّازِ "the house **of the** baker"

Note: The Genitive case causes the preceding noun to be definite as if the article اَلْ were prefixed to it. For example:

بَيْتُ خَبَّازٍ "**the** house of a baker" ;

بَيْتُ الْخَبَّازِ "**the** house of the baker" (and not: بَيْتٌ with a **Tanwin**, because it is definite).

When the preceding noun is indefinite, the preposition لِ must be attached to the following Genitive e. g.

بَيْتٌ لِلْخَبَّازِ "a house of the baker". or :

بَيْتٌ مِنْ بُيُوتِ الْخَبَّازِ "a house of the houses of the baker".

c) The Accusative is expressed by the **Tanwin** ً (an) if the noun is indefinite and by the vowel َ (a) if it is definite. Thus :

هُوَ وَجَدَ كِتَابًا "he found **a** book"

هُوَ وَجَدَ الْكِتَابَ "he found **the** book"

Note: هُوَ وَجَدَ جَرِيدَةً "he found a newspaper" (see above page 33 (36)).

(x) All prepositions are followed by the genitive e.g.: لِخَبَّاز

مِنَ أَلْخَبَّازِ "to (for) a baker"; إِلَى أَلْخَبَّازِ "to the baker";

عَلَى أَلْبَيْتِ "from the baker" (See above page 41, Note);

لِلْخَبَّازِ "on the house"; تَحْتَ أَلْمَائِدَةِ "under the table";

"to (for) the baker" (the ا (Alif) of the article أَلْ falls out if it is

preceded by the preposition لِ e.g. لِلْبَيْتِ instead of (لِأَلْبَيْتِ)

Note 1: بَابُ أَلْبَيْتِ أَلْكَبِيرُ is to be translated:

the big door of the house"

بَابُ أَلْبَيْتِ أَلْكَبِيرِ is to be translated: "the door

of the big house"

Note 2: If a noun in the possessive case (genitive) belongs
to two nouns, it follows the first while the second comes after
it (the genitive) with a possessive-pronoun suffix. For example:

بَيْتُ أَلْخَبَّازِ وَبُسْتَانُهُ "the house of the baker and

his garden" ("the baker's house and garden").

كَرْمُ أَلْجَدَّةِ وَبَيْتُهَا "the vineyard of the grand-mother

and her house" ("the grand-mother's vineyard and house")

Translate: The door of the house; the dog or the
neighbour; the horse is bigger than the ass; he ate bread and
she drank milk; I ate the bread and he drank the milk; this
new house is bigger than that house; the book is on the table;
the dog is under the table; the neighbour is in the vineyard;
your (masc.) house is smaller than this new house; thy (masc.)
newspaper is on the table; thy (fem.) grand-father is in the garden.

Twenty-sixth Lesson

١. مَنْ فَتَحَ اُلْبَابَ اُلْـكَبِيرَ ؟ – أَنَا فَتَحْتُهُ

٢. مَا أَ كَلْتَ اُلْيَوْمَ ؟ – أَ كَلْتُ اُلْيَوْمَ خُبْزاً وَلَحْمًا

٣. كَلْبُ اُلْجَارِ أَسْمَنُ مِنْ كَلْبِ اُلْحَلَّاقِ ٤. أَيْنَ

كِتَابُ مُدِيرِ اُلْمَدْرَسَةِ ؟ – كِتَابُهُ عَلَى اُلْمَائِدَةِ فِي

غُرْفَةِ اُلْجَدِّ ٥. جَدُّ اُلْجَارِ كَانَ اُلْيَوْمَ فِي كَرْمِ أَخِي

٦. جَارُ اُلْخَيَّاطِ فَقِيرٌ. هُوَ أَفْقَرُ مِنْ جَارِ اُلْحَدَّادِ

٧. مَنْ زَارَكَ اُلْيَوْمَ فِي اُلْمَدْرَسَةِ ؟ – مُعَلِّمٌ مُحَمَّدٍ

زَارَنِي هُنَاكَ ٨. مَا اُسْمُكَ وَمَا اُسْمُ أُخْتِكَ ؟ – إِسْمِي

إِسْمَاعِيلُ وَاُسْمُ أُخْتِي فَاطِمَةُ ٩. أُخْتُكَ زَارَتِ اُلْيَوْمَ

أُخْتَ اُلْمُعَلِّمِ ١٠. أَيْنَ اُبْنُ اُلْحَدَّادِ ؟ – إِبْنُهُ فِي بَيْتِ

اُلْخَبَّازِ ١١. أَيْنَ كَلْبُ اُلْخَالِ ؟ – كَلْبُ اُلْخَالِ تَحْتَ

اُلْمَائِدَةِ ١٢. بَيْتُ اُلْخَالَةِ وَكَرْمُهَا ١٣. عَمِّي زَارَ اُلْيَوْمَ

خَالَكَ فِي اُلْبَيْتِ اُلْجَدِيدِ ١٤. عَمَّتِي كَانَتِ اُلْيَوْمَ فِي

كَرْمِ جَدَّتِي ١٥. إِبْنُ اُلْمُعَلِّمِ اُلْكَبِيرِ كَانَ اُلْيَوْمَ

فِي يَافَا ١٦. مَنْ شَرِبَ اُلْحَلِيبَ ؟ – أَنَا مَا شَرِبْتُهُ.

شَرِبَهُ أَخِي إِبْرْهِيمُ .17 خَالِي زَارَ خَالَ الْجَارِ فِي

يَافَا .18 مَا اسْمُ الْخَالِ؟ــ إِسْمُ الْخَالِ إِسْمَاعِيلُ

.19 إِسْمُ أَخِي إِبْرْهِيمُ وَاسْمُ أُخْتِي هِنْدُ .20 هٰذَا

الْبَيْتُ الْجَدِيدُ أَكْبَرُ مِنْ بَيْتِي.

Vocabulary: 115. لَحْمٌ "meat" 116. مُدِيرٌ "director"

117. زَارَ "he visited" (زَارَتْ "she visited") 118. إِسْمٌ "name"

119. إِبْنٌ "son" (The Hamza in إِسْمٌ and in إِبْنٌ is **Hamzat-l-wasl**)

120. سُلَيْمَـانُ "Ismā'īl" (proper noun, masculine) 121. إِسْمَاعِيلُ

"Sulaymān" (proper noun, masculine) 122. خَالٌ "uncle" (on the mother's

side) 123. خَالَةٌ "aunt" (on the mother's side) 124. تَحْتَ "under" (prep.)

125. عَمٌّ "uncle" (on the father's side) 126. عَمَّةٌ "aunt" (on the father's side).

Translate: 1. This dog is big. He is bigger than that
(masc.) dog   2. I have an ass and he has a horse   3. The
horse is bigger than the ass and the camel is bigger than the
horse   4. Where is the director of the school ? — He is in
the room of the grand-father   5. What is thy (masc.) name ?
— my name is Soulaymān   6. I ate bread and meat and she
drank milk 7. This camel is bigger and fatter than that camel
8. The barber is poorer than the blacksmith   9. The teacher
is in the director's room (in the room of the director)   10. The
blacksmith is in the new house   11. This elephant is big. He is
bigger than my elephant   12. Where is the tailor ? — he is in
the house of the baker   13. Where is the new book? — the
new book is on the table.

Twenty-seventh Lesson

١. اَلْأَرْنَبُ حَيَوَانٌ صَغِيرٌ   ٢. أَخِي كَانَ اَلْيَوْمَ فِي حَدِيقَةِ اَلْحَيَوَانَاتِ وَأَبِي يَكُونُ هُنَاكَ غَدًا ٣. مَا رَأَى أَخُوكَ فِي حَدِيقَةِ اَلْحَيَوَانَاتِ؟ ‑ أَخِي رَأَى هُنَاكَ أَسَدًا كَبِيرًا فِي قَفَصٍ كَبِيرٍ   ٤. أَكَتَبْتَ اَلْيَوْمَ ؟ ‑ نَعَمْ كَتَبْتُ اَلْيَوْمَ   ٥. هَلْ فَتَحْتَ بَابَ اَلْكَرْمِ ؟ ‑ لَا مَا فَتَحْتُهُ   ٦. هَلْ يَكُونُ أَخُوكَ غَدًا فِي اَلْمَدْرَسَةِ ؟ ‑ نَعَمْ هُوَ يَكُونُ غَدًا هُنَاكَ ٧. مَا سَأَلْتَ اَلْخَبَّازَ وَمَا أَجَابَ ؟ ‑ سَأَلْتُهُ مَتَى كَانَ فِي بَيْتِ اَلْخَالِ فَأَجَابَ أَنَّهُ كَانَ هُنَاكَ اَلْيَوْمَ   ٨. لِي صَدِيقٌ وَاسْمُهُ سَلِيمٌ   ٩. رَكِبَ أَبِي مَرْكَبًا فِي اَلْبَحْرِ وَأَبُوكَ يَرْكَبُ مَرْكَبًا غَدًا   ١٠. أَخِي رَكِبَ حِمَارًا وَأَخُوكَ رَكِبَ حِصَانًا   ١١. مَاتَ اَلْمَلَّاحُ فِي بَيْتِ صَدِيقِي   ١٢. مَنْ رَأَى أَخَا اَلْمَلَّاحِ ؟ ‑ أَبُو صَدِيقِي رَأَى أَخَا اَلْمَلَّاحِ   ١٣. جَدِّي زَارَ أَبَا اَلْمُعَلِّمِ فِي يَافَا ١٤. اِسْمُ أَبِي اَلْمُعَلِّمِ تَوْفِيقٌ وَاسْمُ أَخِي اَلْمُدِيرِ زَيْدٌ.

<u>Note</u> : The nouns أَبٌ "father"; أَخٌ "brother"; have the following forms before a genitive :

"the father of the neighbour" أَبُو اَلْجَارِ

"the brother of the neighbour" أَخُو اَلْجَارِ

"I saw the father of the neighbour" رَأَيْتُ أَبَا اَلْجَارِ

"I saw the brother of the neighbour" رَأَيْتُ أَخَا اَلْجَارِ

"to the father of the neighbour" إِلَى أَبِي اَلْجَارِ

"to the brother of the neighbour" إِلَى أَخِي اَلْجَارِ

<u>and also</u> : أَبُوكَ "thy (masc.) father"; أَخُوهُ "his brother";

رَأَيْتُ أَخَاهُمْ "I saw thy (masc.) father"; رَأَيْتُ أَبَاكَ "I saw their (masc.) brother"; إِلَى أَبِيكَ "to thy (masc.) father; إِلَى أَخِيكُمْ "to your (masc.) brother".

<u>Vocabulary</u>: 127. (حَيَوَانَاتٌ) "animals" حَيَوَانٌ "animal" 128. حَدِيقَةٌ "garden"; "park" 129. كَانَ "he was" (يَكُونُ) "he will be" or "he is" 130. غَدًا "to-morrow" 131. رَأَى "he saw" (رَأَيْتُ) "I saw" 132. أَسَدٌ "lion" 133. قَفَصٌ "cage" 134. أَ or هَلْ particle of interrogation 135. نَعَمْ "yes" 136. لَا "no"

137. سَأَلَ "to ask" (Imperfect: يَسْأَلُ) 138. أَجَابَ "he answered"

139. فَ "and" "and then" (see page 70 note 2) 140. أَنَّ (أَنِّي "that"

141. أَنَّهُ "that he" etc; أَنَّكَ "that thou (masc.)"; أَنِّي "that I";

142. رَكِبَ "to ride" ; "to sail" ; "to navigate" صَدِيقٌ "a friend"

143. مَرْكَبٌ "a ship" (Note: رَكِبَ مَرْكَبًا، رَكِبَ حِمَارًا

144. بَحْرٌ "a sea" (رَكِبَ (فِي مَرْكَبٍ) عَلَى حِمَارٍ and not:

145. مَاتَ "he died" 146. مَلَّاحٌ "sailor ; "mariner".

Translate: 1. Where is the brother of the director ? — he is in this garden   2. I opened the door of the room 3. Where is my friend ?— thy (masc.) friend is in the room of the grand-father   4. Their (masc.) father was to-day in the school 5. Her father rode an ass and her brother rode a horse 6. My uncle (on the mother's side) visited the father of the teacher 7. Who saw the brother of the tailor ? — the brohter of the blacksmith saw the brother of the tailor 8. The big lion is in a large cage 9. Has he written to-day ?— yes, he has (written)   10. Did he open the door of the room ?— yes, he opened.

Twenty-eighth Lesson

حَارِسُ ٱلْأَسَدِ

كَانَ إِبْرٰهِيمُ فِي حَدِيقَةِ ٱلْحَيَوَانَاتِ وَرَأَى هُنَاكَ أَسَدًا فِي قَفَصٍ كَبِيرٍ . فَسَأَلَ إِبْرٰهِيمُ حَارِسَ ٱلْأَسَدِ: هَلْ أَنْتَ حَارِسُ هٰذَا ٱلْأَسَدِ ٱلْكَبِيرِ ؟

فَأَجَابَ الْحَارِسُ: نَعَمْ

— وَمَنْ يُنَظِّفُ الْقَفَصَ؟— أَنَا.

— أَلَا تَخَافُ مِنَ الْأَسَدِ؟— لَا.

— وَكَيْفَ ذٰلِكَ؟— وَقْتَمَا أُنَظِّفُ هٰذَا الْقَفَصَ يَكُونُ الْأَسَدُ فِي ذٰلِكَ الْقَفَصِ وَوَقْتَمَا أُنَظِّفُ ذٰلِكَ الْقَفَصَ يَكُونُ الْأَسَدُ فِي هٰذَا الْقَفَصِ .

أَسْئِلَةٌ: مَنْ كَانَ فِي حَدِيقَةِ الْحَيَوَانَاتِ؟ مَا رَأَى إِبْرٰهِيمُ فِي حَدِيقَةِ الْحَيَوَانَاتِ؟ مَنْ يُنَظِّفُ قَفَصَ الْأَسَدِ؟ لِمَاذَا لَا يَخَافُ الْحَارِسُ؟

أَحْمَدُ وَالْمَلَّاحُ

سَأَلَ أَحْمَدُ مَلَّاحًا: أَيْنَ مَاتَ أَبُوكَ؟— فَأَجَابَ الْمَلَّاحُ: فِي مَرْكَبٍ كَانَ يَرْكَبُهُ فِي الْبَحْرِ .

وَأَيْنَ مَاتَ جَدُّكَ؟— هُوَ أَيْضًا مَاتَ فِي مَرْكَبٍ كَانَ يَرْكَبُهُ فِي الْبَحْرِ .

— وَلَا تَخَافُ أَنْ تَرْكَبَ مَرْكَبًا بَعْدَ ذٰلِكَ؟

فَقَالَ الْمَلَّاحُ: أَيْنَ مَاتَ أَبُوكَ ؟— عَلَى فِرَاشِهِ.

— وَجَدُّكَ ؟— عَلَى فِرَاشِهِ .

— وَأَنْتَ لَا تَخَافُ أَنْ تَنَامَ عَلَى الْفِرَاشِ بَعْدَ ذٰلِكَ ؟

أَسْئِلَةٌ : مَا سَأَلَ أَحْمَدُ الْمَلَّاحَ ؟ مَا أَجَابَ الْمَلَّاحُ ؟

أَيْنَ مَاتَ جَدُّ الْمَلَّاحِ ؟ مَا سَأَلَ الْمَلَّاحُ أَحْمَدَ ؟

Vocabulary: 147. حَارِس "watchman" 148. نَظَّفَ "to clean"

(أَلَا أُنَظِّفُ) "I shall clean" or "I clean" 149. خَافَ "to fear"

(أَلَا وَقْتٌ) "does he not fear ?" 150. كَيْفَ "how ?" 151. يَخَافُ "time"

(وَقْتَمَا) "while"; "during the time that" 152. سُؤَالٌ "question" (plural:

أَسْئِلَة) 153 لِمَاذَا (and also: لِمَ) " why ? " ; " wherefore ? "

154. فِرَاشٌ "bed", "mattress" 155. نَامَ "to sleep" (أَنَامُ) "I shall sleep" or: "I sleep".

Note 1: فِي مَرْكَبٍ كَانَ يَرْكَبُهُ is to be translated: "in a ship that he sailed".

Note 2: The difference between فَ and وَ is that وَ joins two words or independent sentences, while فَ indicates a development in the narrative e.g بَيْتٌ ; أَكَلَ فَشَرِبَ "he ate and then he drank"; أَكَلَ وَشَرِبَ "he ate and drank", وَكَرْمٌ "a house and a vineyard". In this sentence we do not know if he ate before and then drank, or the contrary. فَ is also used to join two sentences when there is a change of subject

Twenty-nineth Lesson

▪the book▪	(alkitábu) أَلْكِتَابُ
▪the big book▪	(alkitábu-l-kabíru) أَلْكِتَابُ الْكَبِيرُ
▪the copy-book▪	(1) (addáftaru) أَلدَّفْتَرُ
▪the small copy-book▪	(addáftaru-s-saghíru) أَلدَّفْتَرُ الصَّغِيرُ

If the article أَلْ is attached to a noun or adjective which begins with one of the letters ت ث د ذ ر ز س

ش ص ض ط ظ ل ن , then the ل of the article is not pronounced (although it is written) and each of the above letters that follows it, is doubled by **Tashdíd**. For example: أَلدَّفْتَرُ

pronounce: **add**áftaru ▪the copy-book▪; أَلصَّغِيرُ pronounce:

assaghíru ▪the small-; ▪the little▪; أَلدَّفْتَرُ الصَّغِيرُ pronounce:

addáftaru-**s**-saghíru ▪the small copy-book▪.

In this case the ل of the article أَلْ is written without **Sukún**.

١. هٰذَا الدَّفْتَرُ كَبِيرٌ وَذٰلِكَ الدَّفْتَرُ صَغِيرٌ ٢. هٰذَا

الثَّعْلَبُ أَكْبَرُ مِنْ ثَعْلَبِي ٣. مَنْ فَتَحَ الشُّبَّاكَ

الصَّغِيرَ ؟- أَنَا فَتَحْتُ الشُّبَّاكَ الصَّغِيرَ ٤. إِلَى أَينَ

تَذْهَبُ يَا عَمَّتِي ؟ - أَذْهَبُ إِلَى الدُّكَّانِ الْجَدِيدِ

٥. كَانَتْ أُخْتِي فِي السُّوقِ الْجَدِيدِ ٦. ذَهَبْتُ إِلَى

السُّوقِ فِي الصَّبَاحِ وَرَجَعْتُ مِنْ هُنَاكَ فِي الْمَسَاء

٧. كَانَ أَبُو سَلِيمٍ فِي الْمَدْرَسَةِ قَبْلَ الظُّهْرِ ٨. مَا

شَرِبْتَ قَبْلَ الظُّهْرِ وَمَا شَرِبْتَ بَعْدَ الظُّهْرِ ؟ -

شَرِبْتُ قَبْلَ الظُّهْرِ فِنْجَانَ حَلِيبٍ وَبَعْدَ الظُّهْرِ شَرِبْتُ

فِنْجَانَ قَهْوَةٍ ٩. هٰذَا التِّلْمِيذُ أَكْبَرُ مِنْ تِلْمِيذِ

أَخِي ١٠ أَيْنَ الثَّوْرُ السَّمِينُ ؟ - الثَّوْرُ السَّمِينُ فِي

بُسْتَانِ النَّجَّارِ ١١. رَأَى شَاكِرٌ عُصْفُورًا جَمِيلًا عَلَى

الشَّجَرَةِ ١٢. أَخِي شَرِبَ فِنْجَانَ قَهْوَةٍ وَعَمِّي

شَرِبَ حَلِيبًا ١٣. أَيْنَ عُصْفُورُ مُحَمَّدٍ ؟ - عُصْفُورُهُ

فِي قَفَصٍ صَغِيرٍ ١٤. لِي ثَعْلَبٌ وَأَرْنَبٌ وَلَكَ

كَلْبٌ وَخَرُوفٌ ١٥. أَيْنَ الْعُصْفُورُ الصَّغِيرُ ؟ -

الْعُصْفُورُ الصَّغِيرُ عَلَى الشَّجَرَةِ ١٦. أَيْنَ الْكُرْسِيُّ

الْجَدِيدُ ؟ - الْكُرْسِيُّ الْجَدِيدُ تَحْتَ الشَّجَرَةِ .

Vocabulary:

156. ثَعْلَب "fox" 157. دُكَّان "shop"

158. سُوق "market" 159. صَبَاح "morning" 160. مَسَاء "evening"

161. قَبْلَ "before" (prep.) 162. بَعْدَ "after" (prep.) 163. ظُهْر

"midday" (بَعْدَ الظُّهْر "fore-noon", قَبْلَ الظُّهْر "after-noon"

64. قَهْوَة "coffee" 165. نَجَّار "joiner"; "carpenter" 166. عُصْفُور

"bird" 167. جَمِيل "beautiful", "pretty" 168. شَجَرَة "tree".

Translate:

1. I drank a cup of coffee and my sister drank milk 2. My brother was in the new shop 3. My grand-father was in the school and returned from there in the after-noon 4. Her sister was in the market in the morning 5. Where is the small bird? — it is on the tree in the garden 6. I have a fox and he has a fox 7. This fox is fatter than that fox 8. This ox is bigger than that ox 9. Where is your (masc.) pupil?— he is in the room of the grand-father 10. Where is the house of the tailor?— the house of the tailor is in the market 11. Where is the carpenter?— the carpenter is in the garden of the baker 12. This carpenter is poorer than that carpenter 13. This bird is bigger than that bird 14. My brother was in the school in the morning and my sister was there in the after-noon.

Thirtieth Lesson

أَمْثَالٌ

١. كَلْبٌ حَيٌّ خَيْرٌ مِنْ أَسَدٍ مَيْتٍ

٢. عَدُوٌّ عَاقِلٌ خَيْرٌ مِنْ صَدِيقٍ جَاهِلٍ

٣. عُصْفُورٌ فِي الْيَدِ وَلَا عَشَرَةٌ عَلَى الشَّجَرَهْ

٤. سَلَامَةُ الْإِنْسَانِ فِي حِفْظِ اللِّسَانِ

أَلْمُعَلِّمُ وَتِلْمِيذُهُ الرَّسَّامُ

قَالَ الْمُعَلِّمُ لِسَلِيمٍ : أُرْسُمْ يَا سَلِيمْ عَلَى اللَّوْحِ حِمَارًا بَرْكَبُهُ وَلَدٌ. فَرَسَمَ سَلِيمٌ عَلَى اللَّوْحِ حِمَارًا وَمَا رَسَمَ الْوَلَدَ.

أَلْمُعَلِّمُ: وَأَيْنَ الْوَلَدُ ؟ — سَلِيمٌ: نَزَلَ يَا مُعَلِّمِي.

أَسْئِلَةٌ : مَا قَالَ الْمُعَلِّمُ لِسَلِيمٍ ؟ مَا رَسَمَ سَلِيمٌ ؟

مَا سَأَلَ الْمُعَلِّمُ سَلِيمًا ؟ مَا أَجَابَ سَلِيمٌ ؟

Vocabulary: 169. مَثَلٌ (plural: أَمْثَالٌ) "example",
"proverb" 170. حَيُّ "alive" 171. طَيِّبٌ or جَيِّدٌ "good" (خَيْرٌ مِنْ
"better than") 172. مَيِّتٌ or مَيْتٌ "dead" 173. عَدُوٌّ "enemy",
"foe" 174. عَاقِلٌ "intelligent" 175. جَاهِلٌ "ignorant", "foolish"
176. سَلَامَةٌ "security", "safety" 177. عَشَرَةٌ "ten" 178. يَدٌ "hand"
179. حِفْظٌ "keeping" 180. إِنْسَانٌ "man", person" 181. رَسَّامٌ
"draughtsman" 182. لِسَانٌ "tongue", "language" 183. لَوْحٌ "blackboard"
184. رَسَمَ imperative of أُرْسُمْ
185. نَزَلَ "to descend".

Thirty-first Lesson

"a big brother"	أَخٌ كَبِيرٌ
"a big sister"	أُخْتٌ كَبِيرَةٌ
"a new book"	كِتَابٌ جَدِيدٌ
"a new newspaper"	جَرِيدَةٌ جَدِيدَةٌ
"a clean hand"	يَدٌ نَظِيفَةٌ

In Arabic there are two genders: masculine and feminine.

Normally the male is masculine and the female is feminine

e. g. أَبٌ "father", أُمٌّ "mother".

But in Arabic the genders in grammar must not be connected with the sexes: things without life, and without sex are still treated as masculine or feminine.

The nouns which denote inanimate things are feminine:

) when they end in ة. For example: جَرِيدَةٌ "a newspaper";

سَفِينَةٌ "a ship".

) when they are names of lands and cities. For example: مِصْرُ "Egypt", "Cairo"; يَافَا "Jaffa".

) when they denote the parts of the body which are in pairs.

For example: يَدٌ "hand"; رِجْلٌ "foot"; عَيْنٌ "eye" etc.

Note: The following nouns are feminine without a special ending:

أَرْضٌ "earth", بِئْرٌ "well", حَرْبٌ "war", خَمْرٌ "wine",

دَارٌ "house"، رِيحٌ "wind"، شَمْسٌ "sun".

If the noun is feminine, the descriptive adjective which follows it must be feminine also, the feminine being usually formed by adding the ending ة to the masculine.. For example

غُرْفَةٌ نَظِيفَةٌ "a clean room" (كِتَابٌ نَظِيفٌ)،

سَفِينَةٌ صَغِيرَةٌ "a small ship" (بَيْتٌ صَغِيرٌ).

1. مَتَى طَلَعَ أَخُوكَ الْجَبَلَ وَمَتَى نَزَلَ مِنْهُ ؟
- أَخِي طَلَعَ الْجَبَلَ قَبْلَ الظُّهْرِ 2. مَا أَكَلَ أَخُوكَ
وَمَا أَكَلَتْ أُخْتُكَ ؟- أَخِي أَكَلَ خُبْزاً وَقِطْعَةَ
لَحْمٍ وَأُخْتِي أَكَلَتْ خُبْزاً وَقِطْعَةَ جُبْنٍ 3. أَيْنَ
هِرَّةُ خَالَتِي ؟- هِيَ فِي الْغُرْفَةِ الصَّغِيرَةِ 4. لِجَدَّتِي هِرَّةٌ
وَقِرْدٌ. اَلْقِرْدُ أَكْبَرُ مِنَ الْهِرَّةِ 5. هٰذِهِ الْيَدُ
نَظِيفَةٌ وَتِلْكَ الْيَدُ وَسِخَةٌ 6. هٰذِهِ الرَّجْلُ نَظِيفَةٌ
وَتِلْكَ الرَّجْلُ وَسِخَةٌ 7. مَنْ أَخَذَ جَرِيدَةَ الْمُعَلِّمِ ؟-
لَا أَعْرِفُ مَنْ أَخَذَهَا 8. هَلْ تَعْرِفُ أَخَا سَلِيمٍ ؟- لَا،
لَا أَعْرِفُهُ 9. مَنْ رَفَعَ هٰذِهِ الْجَرِيدَةَ مِنَ الْأَرْضِ ؟-

أَنَا رَفَعْتُهَا .10 وَجَدَ أَخِي جَوْزَةً عَلَى الْأَرْضِ فَرَفَعَهَا

.11 سَلِيمٌ رَفَعَ هٰذِهِ الْجَـوْزَةَ مِنَ الْأَرْضِ .12 أَيْنَ

جَرِيدَةُ أَخِي ؟– أَخَذَهَا إِبْرٰهِيمُ وَوَضَعَهَا عَلَى الْمَائِدَةِ

الْـكَبِيرَةِ .13 أَيْنَ أَخِي الصَّغِيرُ ؟– هُوَ فِي الْغَابَةِ

.14 أَخُوكَ يَلْعَبُ مَعَ أَخِي فِي الْغَابَةِ .15 لَعِبَ

أَحْمَدُ مَعَ أَخِي فِي الْغَابَةِ.

Vocabulary: 186. طَلَعَ "to mount", "to rise", "to go up"

187. جَبَلٌ "mountain", "mount· 188. قِطْعَةٌ "a piece" 189. جُبْنٌ

"cheese" 190. هِرَّةٌ "cat" 191. هِرَّةٌ "a she-cat" 192. قِرْدٌ "ape";

"monkey" 193. هٰذِهِ "this (fem.)" 194. تِلْكَ "that (fem.)"

"that cow") تِلْكَ الْبَقَرَةُ "this cow", هٰذِهِ الْبَقَرَةُ (

195. رِجْلٌ "foot· 196. وَسِخٌ "dirty" 197. نَظِيفٌ "clean"

198. أَخَذَ "to take" 199. عَرَفَ "to know" (Imperf. أَعْرِفُ)

200 رَفَعَ "to lift up" (Imperf. أَرْفَعُ) 201. أَرْضٌ "earth·, "land·

202. جَوْزَةٌ "nut· 203. وَضَعَ "to lay", "to put· 204. غَابَةٌ "forest·

205. لَعِبَ "to play· (Imperf. أَلْعَبُ).

Translate: 1. This school is small and that school is big 2. Where is the she-cat of the sister? — her she-cat is in that room 3. This room is big and that room is small 4. Does thy (masc.) brother know where is the director of this school? — no, he does not know where he is 5. This foot is clean and that foot is dirty 6. The room of the sister is clean and the room of the brother is dirty 7. This cow is fat 8. That dog is bigger than this dog 9. That cow is big and this cow is small 10. Who was in this room and who was in that room? — Thy (masc.) brother was in this room and his brother was in that room.

Thirty-second Lesson
A

"two big asses" (1)	حِمَارَانِ كَبِيرَانِ
	حِمَارٌ كَبِيرٌ "a big ass"
"the two big asses"	أَلْحِمَارَانِ الْكَبِيرَانِ
"these two big asses"	هٰذَانِ الْحِمَارَانِ
"two big cows" (2)	بَقَرَتَانِ كَبِيرَتَانِ
	بَقَرَةٌ كَبِيرَةٌ "a big cow"
"these two cows"	هٰتَانِ الْبَقَرَتَانِ

(1) There are three numbers in Arabic : Singular, Dual (which denotes the number **two** of things) and Plural (see below page 90).

The Dual is expressed by adding of the termination انِ to the singular, thus :

"the two dogs", كَلْبَانِ "two dogs", (كَلْبٌ "a dog"); أَلْكَلْبَانِ

كَلْبَانِ كَبِيرَانِ "two big dogs", هٰذَانِ

الْكَلْبَانِ "these two dogs .

(2) **Nouns** ending in ة (Tā Marbuṭa see above 31 (33)) change the ة

into · تْ (Tā Ṭawīla) before the Dual-termination e. g. بَقَرَتَانِ

"two cows" (بَقَرَةٌ "a cow") ; بَقَرَتَانِ كَبِيرَتَانِ "two big

cows" ; هٰتَانِ الْبَقَرَتَانِ "these two cows".

B

"the possessor of **two** asses" (1)	صَاحِبُ حِمَارَيْنِ كَبِيرَيْنِ
"from these **two** asses"	مِنْ هٰذَيْنِ الْحِمَارَيْنِ
"on these **two** cows"	عَلَى هٰتَيْنِ الْبَقَرَتَيْنِ
"I saw the **two** big asses"	رَأَيْتُ الْحِمَارَيْنِ الْكَبِيرَيْنِ
"I saw these **two** cows"	رَأَيْتُ هٰتَيْنِ الْبَقَرَتَيْنِ

1) The Dual takes the termination انِ ‾ for the Nominative and the

termination يْنِ ‾ for both the Genitive and the Accusative

(see above lesson 25) e. g. :

الْكَلْبَانِ فِي الْبُسْتَانِ "the **two** dogs are in the garden"

صَاحِبُ الْبَيْتَيْنِ "the possessor of the **two** houses"

فِي الْبَيْتَيْنِ "in the **two** houses"

رَأَيْتُ الْبَقَرَتَيْنِ "I saw the **two** cows"

رَأَيْتُ هٰتَيْنِ الْبَقَرَتَيْنِ "I saw these **two** cows"

C

"the **two** asses of the baker"	(1) حِمَارَا اَلْخَبَّازِ
"the **two** big asses of the baker"	حِمَارَا اَلْخَبَّازِ اَلْكَبِيرَانِ
"his **two** asses"	حِمَارَاهُ
"his **two** big asses"	حِمَارَاهُ اَلْكَبِيرَانِ
"on the **two** asses of my brother"	عَلَى حِمَارَيْ أَخِي
"from thy (masc.) **two** asses"	مِنْ حِمَارَيْكَ
"I saw thy (masc.) **two** asses"	رَأَيْتُ حِمَارَيْكَ

(1) The final نِ (ni) of the Dual-termination falls out when the Dual is followed by the Genitive. For example:

"the **two** asses of the baker" حِمَارَا اَلْخَبَّازِ

"in the **two** gardens of my brother" فِي بُسْتَانَيْ أَخِي

"I saw the **two** asses of my brother" رَأَيْتُ حِمَارَيْ أَخِي

"the **two** big cows of the baker" بَقَرَتَا اَلْخَبَّازِ اَلْكَبِيرَتَانِ

(see above page 63, note 1).

<u>and also</u>: حِمَارَاكَ "thy (masc.) **two** asses";

حِمَارَاهُ اَلْكَبِيرَانِ "his **two** big asses";

رَأَيْتُ حِمَارَيْكَ "I saw thy (masc.) **two** asses".

Note 1: كَتَبْتُمَا "you (masc. and fem.) **two** have written" (see above page 28).

كَتَبَا "they (masc.) **two** have written" (see above).

كَتَبَتَا "they (fem.) **two** have written" (see above).

Note 2: تَكْتُبَانِ "you (masc. and fem.) **two** will write" or: "you **two** write" (see above page 48).

يَكْتُبَانِ "they (masc. and fem.) **two** will write" or: "they **two** write".

For the first person there is no special Dual form e. g. كَتَبْنَا "we **two** have written" or: "we (more than two) have written" (see above p. 28), نَكْتُبُ "we **two** shall write" or: "we (more than two) shall write" (see above page 48).

Note 3: لَكُمَا "you (masc. and fem.) **two** have" (see above page 15).

لَهُمَا "they (masc. and fem.) **two** have".

كِتَابُكُمَا "your (Dual masc. and fem.) book".

كِتَابُهُمَا "their (Dual masc. and fem.) book" (see above page 22).

Thirty-third Lesson

١. لِي ثَوْرَانِ كَبِيرَانِ وَلَكَ بَقَرَتَانِ كَبِيرَتَا

٢. كَلْبَا أَخِي كَبِيرَانِ وَ كَلْبَا جَدِّي صَغِيرَانِ ٣. بَقَرَتَا

صَغِيرَتَانِ وَبَقَرَتَاهُ كَبِيرَتَانِ   ٤. أَخِي قَسَمَ قِطْعَةَ

الْجُبْنِ إِلَى قِسْمَيْنِ. هُوَ أَكَلَ الْقِسْمَ الْأَوَّلَ وَأُخْتِي

أَكَلَتِ الْقِسْمَ الْآخَرَ   ٥. إِشْتَرَيْتُ الْيَوْمَ بَقَرَتَيْنِ.

بَقَرَةً وَاحِدَةً قَبْلَ الظُّهْرِ وَبَقَرَةً وَاحِدَةً بَعْدَ الظُّهْرِ.

الْبَقَرَةُ الْأُولَى صَغِيرَةٌ وَالْأُخْرَى كَبِيرَةٌ   ٦. هٰذَا

الْخَيَّاطُ كَبِيرُ السِّنّ. هُوَ أَكْبَرُ سِنًّا مِنْ ذٰلِكَ

الْخَيَّاطِ   ٧. هٰذَانِ الْكَلْبَانِ صَغِيرَانِ وَهٰتَانِ الْبَقَرَتَانِ

كَبِيرَتَانِ   ٨. أَلْخُبْزُ الَّذِي اشْتَرَيْتَ فِي السُّوقِ

الْجَدِيدِ أَرْخَصُ مِنَ الْخُبْزِ الَّذِي اشْتَرَيْتُ فِي

ذٰلِكَ الدُّكَّانِ   ٩. مَنْ فَلَقَ الْجَوْزَةَ الَّتِي كَانَتْ عَلَى

الْمَائِدَةِ فِي غُرْفَتِي وَمَنْ أَكَلَ لُبَّهَا ؟- سَلِيمٌ فَلَقَهَا

وَأَكَلَ لُبَّهَا   ١٠. هٰذَانِ الْكَرْمَانِ أَكْبَرُ مِنْ

كَرْمَيْ أَخِي   ١١. هٰتَانِ الْجَرِيدَتَانِ أَكْبَرُ مِنْ

جَرِيدَتَيْ زَيْدٍ   ١٢. هٰذَانِ الْحِمَارَانِ أَصْغَرُ مِنْ

حِمَارَيْكَ   ١٣. لَنَا كَرْمَانِ وَلَكُمْ بَيْتَانِ.

<u>Vocabulary</u>: 206 قَسَمَ "to divide" (Imperf يَقْسِمُ)

207. قِسْمٌ "part" 208 أَوَّلُ "first" (fem أُولَى) 209. آخَرُ "other"

210. إِشْتَرَى "he bought" (إِشْتَرَيْتُ "I bought", أُخْرَى fem.)

(إِشْتَرَيْتَ، إِشْتَرَيْتِ etc the **Hamza** in this word is **Hamzat-l-wasl**)

211. وَاحِدٌ "one" (fem. وَاحِدَةٌ) 212. سِنٌّ "age", "tooth"

213 كَبِيرُ السِّنّ "old" (أَكْبَرُ سِنًّا مِنْ) "older than")

214. هٰذَانِ "these two" (fem. هٰتَانِ) 215. أَلَّذِي "which", "who"

217. فَلَقَ "to split" 216. لُبٌّ "marrow", "core" (أَلَّتِي fem.)

<u>Note</u> : أَكْبَرُ "is (masc. and fem.) bigger" and also : "are (masc. and fem.) bigger"

Thirty-fourth Lesson

١. قَسَمَ إِبْرٰهِيمُ قِطْعَةَ اللَّحْمِ إِلَى قِسْمَيْنِ. ثُمَّ وَضَعَ كُلَّ وَاحِدٍ مِنَ الْقِسْمَيْنِ فِي كَفَّةٍ مِنَ الْمِيزَانِ

٢. مِيزَانُ أَخِي أَكْبَرُ مِنْ مِيزَانِ جَدِّكَ ٣. مَا فَعَلْتَ بِالسُّكَّرِ الَّذِي اشْتَرَيْتَ فِي السُّوقِ الْجَدِيدِ؟

- قَسَمْتُهُ أَوَّلًا إِلَى قِسْمَيْنِ ثُمَّ وَضَعْتُ كُلَّ وَاحِدٍ مِنَ الْقِسْمَيْنِ عَلَى الْمَائِدَةِ فِي غُرْفَتِي ٤. لِأَخِي

ثَوْرَانِ سَمِينَانِ وَلِي بَقَرَتَانِ سَمِيْنَتَانِ ٥. قَالَ أَبُوكَ

لِأَخِيكَ أَرْسُمْ لِي سَيَّارَتَيْنِ فَرَسَمَ أَخُوكَ سَيَّارَتَيْنِ

٦. ذَهَبَ أَخِي وَأُخْتِي إِلَى الْمَدْرَسَةِ قَبْلَ الظُّهْرِ

وَرَجَعَا مِنْ هُنَاكَ بَعْدَ الظُّهْرِ ٧. أَيْنَ أُخْتِي وَأُخْتُكَ؟

ـ هُمَا ذَهَبَتَا إِلَى الْمَدْرَسَةِ ٨. مِنْ أَيْنَ رَجَعْنَا أَنَا وَأَخِي؟

ـ أَنْتُمَا رَجَعْتُمَا مِنَ الْمَدْرَسَةِ ٩. هَذَا الْكِتَابُ

رَخِيصٌ وَذَلِكَ الْكِتَابُ أَرْخَصُ مِنْهُ بِقَلِيلٍ ١٠. أَنَا

شَرِبْتُ قَلِيلاً مِنَ الْحَلِيبِ وَأَكَلْتُ قَلِيلاً مِنَ

الْخُبْزِ وَأَخِي أَكَلَ وَشَرِبَ أَكْثَرَ مِنِّي ١١. بَيْتَا أَخِي

الْجَدِيدَانِ أَكْبَرُ مِنْ بَيْتَيْ سَلِيمٍ بِكَثِيرٍ ١٢. أُخْتَا

سَلِيمٍ كَتَبَتَا وَقَرَأَتَا الْيَوْمَ كَثِيراً ١٣. مَا ذَهَبْتُ

الْيَوْمَ إِلَى الْمَدْرَسَةِ لِأَنَّ أَبِي مَرِيضٌ ١٤. أَخِي مَا

ذَهَبَ الْيَوْمَ إِلَى الْمَدْرَسَةِ لِأَنَّهُ مَرِيضٌ. ١٥. مَا

أَكَلْتَ قَبْلَ الظُّهْرِ؟ ـ أَكَلْتُ خُبْزًا وَقِطْعَةَ لَحْمٍ

Vocabulary:

218 ثُمَّ "then", 219 كُلّ "all", "whole", "every" (أَلْبَيْتُ كُلُّهُ or : كُلُّ ٱلْبَيْتِ "the whole house"—

(كُلُّ بَيْتٍ كُلّ makes the next noun to be in the genitive e. g.

220 كَفَّة "a scale of a balance", 221 مِيزَان "balance",

222 فَعَلَ "to do", 223 بِ "with"; "by", "in", (بِی "with me",

بِكَ، بِكِ etc. (see above page 15) 224 سُكَّر "sugar", 225 أَوَّلًا

"firstly", 226 سَيَّارَة "automobile", 227 هُمَا "they (Dual masc. and

fem.)", 228 أَنْتُمَا "you (Dual masc and fem.)", 229 قَلِيل "a little",

230 كَثِير "much", (أَكْثَرُ مِنْ "more than"); 231 لِأَنَّ

"because", 232 مَرِيض "ill," "sick". 233 قَالَ "he said",

(أَقُولُ Imperfect :

Translate:

1. The two dogs of my brother are in the garden of thy (masc.) sister   2. The two big hares are in the vineyard of the uncle (on the father's side)   3. I have two houses and my father too has two houses. His two houses are in the new market.   4. The two cows of my grand-mother are fatter than the two cows of the tailor   5. Where are the two newspapers of the director ? — They (two) are on the table in the room of the father   6. The house of the baker and his garden   7. Her two oxen are bigger than his two oxen   8. The two dogs of the tailor and his two hares   9. The two asses of my aunt (on the mother's side) and her two camels   10. He has one ass and two oxen and we have two asses and one ox.

Thirty-fifth Lesson

هِرَّتَانِ وَقِرْدٌ

هِرَّتَانِ وَجَدَتَا قِطْعَةَ جُبْنٍ وَذَهَبَتَا بِهَا إِلَى ٱلْقِرْدِ
كَيْ يَقْسِمَهَا بَيْنَهُمَا. فَأَخَذَ ٱلْقِرْدُ ٱلْجُبْنَةَ وَقَسَمَهَا
لَى قِسْمَيْنِ أَحَدُهُمَا أَكْبَرُ مِنَ ٱلْآخَرِ. ثُمَّ وَضَعَ كُلَّ
احِدٍ مِنَ ٱلْقِسْمَيْنِ فِي كَفَّةٍ مِنْ مِيزَانِهِ . فَرَجَحَ
قِسْمُ ٱلْأَكْبَرُ. فَأَخَذَ مِنْهُ قَلِيلًا بِأَسْنَانِهِ وَأَكَلَهُ
قَالَ: أُرِيدُ أَنْ أُسَاوِيَهُ بِٱلْأَصْغَرِ. وَلٰكِنْ إِذْ كَانَ
ا أَخَذَهُ مِنْهُ أَكْثَرَ مِنَ ٱللَّازِمِ رَجَحَ ٱلْأَصْغَرُ.
فَعَلَ بِهٰذَا مَا فَعَلَهُ بِذٰلِكَ ثُمَّ فَعَلَ بِذٰلِكَ مَا فَعَلَهُ
ٰذَا وَمَا زَالَ يَأْكُلُ مِمَّا رَجَحَ مِنَ ٱلْقِسْمَيْنِ حَتَّى
كَلَ ٱلْجُبْنَةَ كُلَّهَا.

سْئِلَةٌ: أَلْهِرَّتَانِ مَا وَجَدَتَا؟ إِلَى مَنْ ذَهَبَتَا؟
ِاذَا ذَهَبَتَا بِٱلْجُبْنَةِ إِلَى ٱلْقِرْدِ؟ مَا فَعَلَ ٱلْقِرْدُ
ْجُبْنَةَ؟ فِي مَا وَضَعَ كُلَّ وَاحِدٍ مِنَ ٱلْقِسْمَيْنِ؟

لِمَاذَا رَجَحَ أَحَدُ ٱلْقِسْمَيْنِ؟ لِمَاذَا أُكِلَ مِنَ ٱلْقِسْمِ
ٱلْأَكْبَرِ؟ لِمَاذَا أُكِلَ مِنَ ٱلْقِسْمِ ٱلْآخَرِ؟ هَلْ
بَقِيَ شَيْءٌ مِنَ ٱلْجُبْنَةِ؟

Vocabulary: 234. كَيْ "in order that" (كَيْ يَقْسِمَ
"in order that he divide") 235. بَيْنَ "between" 236. جُبْنَةٌ "a
piece of cheese" 237. رَجَحَ "to outweigh" 238. أَحَدُهُمَا "one of them (dual)"
"to outweigh" 239. سِنٌّ "tooth" (plural: أَسْنَانٌ) 240. أَرَادَ "to
wish", "to desire" (Imperfect: أُرِيدُ) 241. سَاوَى "to make equal"
242. (أُسَاوِي : Imperfect) لَـكِنْ، لٰكِنَّ، وَلٰكِنْ or وَلٰكِنَّ)
"but" 243. إِذْ (followed by a verb) "since", "because" 244. لَازِمٌ
"necessary" 245. زَالَ "to cease" 246. مِمَّا = مِنْ مَا 247. حَتَّى "until".

Thirty-sixth Lesson

أَلْوَلَدَانِ وَٱلْجَوْزَةُ

وَلَدَانِ صَغِيرَانِ وَجَدَا جَوْزَةً تَحْتَ شَجَرَةِ جَوْزٍ
فَقَالَ أَحَدُهُمَا: هٰذِهِ جَوْزَتِي لِأَنِّي رَأَيْتُهَا أَوَّلًا. فَقَالَ
ٱلثَّانِي: لَا بَلْ هِيَ لِي لِأَنِّي رَفَعْتُهَا مِنَ ٱلْأَرْضِ.

فَتَشَاجَرَ عَلَى ذٰلِكَ مُشَاجَرَةً شَدِيدَةً. وَبَيْنَمَا هُمَا فِي هٰذِهِ الْمُشَاجَرَةِ فَإِذَا بِوَلَدٍ آخَرَ قَدْ تَقَرَّبَ مِنْهُمَا. وَكَانَ هٰذَا الْوَلَدُ أَكْبَرَ مِنْهُمَا سِنًّا وَقَالَ لَهُمَا: أَنَا أُوَفِّقُ بَيْنَكُمَا. فَوَقَفَ بَيْنَهُمَا وَبَعْدَ مَا سَمِعَ طَلِبَةَ كُلِّ وَاحِدٍ مِنْهُمَا فَلَقَ الْجَوْزَةَ وَقَالَ: الْقِشْرَةُ الْأُولَى لِمَنْ رَأَى الْجَوْزَةَ أَوَّلًا وَالْقِشْرَةُ الْأُخْرَى لِمَنْ رَفَعَهَا مِنَ الْأَرْضِ. أَمَّا اللُّبُّ فَهُوَ لِي جَزَاءُ الْقَضَاءِ.

أَسْئِلَةٌ: الْوَلَدَانِ الصَّغِيرَانِ مَا وَجَدَا؟ أَيْنَ وَجَدَا الْجَوْزَةَ؟ مَا قَالَ أَحَدُهُمَا وَمَا قَالَ الْآخَرُ؟ مَتَى تَقَرَّبَ مِنْهُمَا وَلَدٌ آخَرُ؟ أَكَانَ هٰذَا الْوَلَدُ أَصْغَرَ سِنًّا مِنْهُمَا؟ مَا قَالَ لَهُمَا؟ بَعْدَ مَا سَمِعَ طَلِبَةَ كُلِّ وَاحِدٍ مِنْهُمَا مَا فَعَلَ؟ كَيْفَ وَفَّقَ بَيْنَهُمَا؟

Vocabulary: 248. الثَّانِي "the second" 249. جَوْزٌ "nut" 250. بَلْ "but" 251. تَشَاجَرَ "to quarrel" 252. مُشَاجَرَةٌ "quarrel"

253. شَدِيدٌ "strong"; "violent" 254. بَيْنَمَا "while" 255. إِذَا (followed

by a verb) "when"; "if" 256. إِذَا بِ "see!"; "behold!"

قَدْ مَاتَ) "Behold, an ox died" 257. قَدْ is a particle which is often put before

the perfect to express the completion or certainty of the action and can sometimes

be translated "already" but often it is to be left untranslated 258. تَقَرَّبَ مِنْ

"to approach" 259. وَفَّقَ (بَيْن) "to reconcile" (Imperf. : أُوَفِّقُ)

260. وَقَفَ "to stand" 261. سَمِعَ "to hear" (Imperfect : أَسْمَعُ)

262. طِلْبَةٌ "demand"; "request" 263. قِشْرَةٌ "rind"; "shell" 264. أَمَّا

"as for"; "as to" 265. جَزَاءٌ "reward" 266. قَضَاءٌ "judgment".

Translate:

1. My brother stood between the grandfather and the sister   2. What did he hear in the room of the director ?— he heard there that thou (masc.) art ill   3. My sister took the meat and divided it in two parts   4. Where is the new book which I bought in the new shop ? — thy (masc.) sister put it on the new table   5. thy (fem.) two cows are fatter than the two cows of my grand-mother   6. His two houses are nearer than thy (masc.) two houses   7. I have two new books and he too has two new books   8. Where are the two asses ?— They (dual) are in the garden   9. Where are the two new houses of the tailor ? — they (dual) are in the new market   10. We have two oxen and she also has two oxen. 11. My two asses are bigger than the two asses of my brother. 12. When did thy (masc.) teacher visit our uncle (on the mother's side) ? — he visited him in the after-noon   13. Her grand-mother visited to-day the mother of the teacher   14. Where did you (masc.) learn the Arabic language ?— I learned it in school.

Thirty-seventh Lesson

A

"bakers"	خَبَّازُونَ (1)
"the bakers"	أَلْخَبَّازُونَ
"these bakers"	هٰؤُلَاءِ الْخَبَّازُونَ
"the house of the bakers"	بَيْتُ الْخَبَّازِينَ (2)
"I saw the bakers"	رَأَيْتُ الْخَبَّازِينَ
"the teachers of my brother"	مُعَلِّمُو أَخِي (3)
"to the teachers of my brother"	إِلَى مُعَلِّمِي أَخِي
"I saw the teachers of my brother"	رَأَيْتُ مُعَلِّمِي أَخِي
"thy (masc.) teachers"	مُعَلِّمُوكَ
"the room of thy (masc.) teachers"	غُرْفَةُ مُعَلِّمِيكَ
"I saw thy (masc) teachers"	رَأَيْتُ مُعَلِّمِيكَ

(1) The plural of masculines is formed by adding to the singular the termination ُونَ thus: خَبَّازُونَ "bakers" (خَبَّازٌ "baker")

(2) The plural of masculines has the termination ُونَ for the Nominative and the termination ِينَ for the Genitive and

Accusative (See above Lesson 32 B. (1)) e. g.

أَلْخَبَّازُونَ فِي الْبُسْتَانِ "the bakers are in the garden";

بَيْتُ الْخَبَّازِينَ "the house of the bakers";

رَأَيْتُ الْخَبَّازِينَ "I saw the bakers".

(3) The final نَ (na) of the plural masculine termination is omitted when the plural is followed by a genitive e. g.

مُعَلِّمُو أَخِي "the teachers of my brother" (and also:

مُعَلِّمُوا أَخِي with an Alif (١) after the (و);

غُرْفَةُ مُعَلِّمِي أَخِي "the room of the teachers of my brother";

رَأَيْتُ مُعَلِّمِي أَخِي "I saw the teachers of my brother".

and also: مُعَلِّمُوهُ "his teachers"; غُرْفَةُ مُعَلِّمِيكَ "the room of thy (masc.) teachers" etc.

B

"(female) teachers"	مُعَلِّمَاتٌ (1)
"the (female) teachers"	أَلْمُعَلِّمَاتُ
"from the (female) teachers"	مِنَ الْمُعَلِّمَاتِ (2)
"her (female) teachers"	مُعَلِّمَاتُهَا

(1) The plural of feminine nouns is formed by changing ةٌ

into اَت e.g. مُعَلِّمَاتٌ "(female) teachers" (singular: مُعَلِّمَةٌ)

(2) The plural of the feminines has the termination اَتٌ for the Nominative and the termination اَتِ for the Genitive and Accusative e. g.

اَلْمُعَلِّمَاتُ فِي الْغُرْفَةِ "the (female) teachers are in the room";

غُرْفَةُ الْمُعَلِّمَاتِ "the room of the (female) teachers";

رَأَيْتُ الْمُعَلِّمَاتِ "I saw the (female) teachers".

Note : There are some feminine nouns which take the plural termination of the masculine nouns and some masculine nouns which take the plural termination of the feminines e. g. حَيَوَانَاتٌ "animals" ; (سَنَةٌ : singular) "years" سِنُونَ (حَيَوَانٌ : singular).

Thirty-eighth Lesson

١. اَلْمُسْلِمُونَ لَا يَشْرَبُونَ خَمْرًا وَلَا يَأْكُلُونَ لَحْمَ الْخِنْزِيرِ ٢. مُعَلِّمُوا مَدْرَسَتِي وَمُعَلِّمَاتُهَا زَارُوا قَبْلَ الظُّهْرِ الْجَامِعَ الَّذِي فِي حَارَةِ الْحَدَّادِينَ ٣. أَيْنَ تَعَلَّمَ أَخُوكَ اللُّغَةَ الْعَرَبِيَّةَ؟ - أَخِي تَعَلَّمَ اللُّغَةَ الْعَرَبِيَّةَ فِي الْمَدْرَسَةِ الَّتِي فِي شَارِعِ يَافَا ٤. أَتَعَلَّمْتَ

فِي الْمَدْرَسَةِ اللُّغَةَ الْإِنْكِلِيزِيَّةَ ؟- نَعَمْ تَعَلَّمْتُهَا

هُنَاكَ ٥. مَا هِيَ الْجِهَاتُ الْأَرْبَعُ ؟- الْجِهَاتُ

الْأَرْبَعُ هِيَ الشَّرْقُ وَالْغَرْبُ وَالشِّمَالُ وَالْجَنُوبُ

٦. مَا تَعَلَّمْتَ الْيَوْمَ فِي الْمَدْرَسَةِ ؟- تَعَلَّمْتُ الْيَوْمَ

الْجِهَاتِ الْأَرْبَعَ ٧. مُعَلِّمُوكَ زَارُوا مُعَلِّمِي أَخِي

فِي الْمَدْرَسَةِ ٨. أَيْنَ أَخُو الْجَارِ الصَّغِيرُ ؟- هُوَ

يَلْعَبُ الْآنَ أَمَامَ الْبُسْتَانِ وَيَصِيحُ بِصَوْتٍ عَالٍ

٩. مَنْ صَاحَ أَمَامَ الْبَيْتِ قَبْلَ الظُّهْرِ ؟- أَخُو الْجَارِ

الصَّغِيرُ لَعِبَ وَصَاحَ أَمَامَ الْبَيْتِ ١٠. هٰؤُلَاءِ

الْمُعَلِّمُونَ كَانُوا الْيَوْمَ فِي الْغَابَةِ وَأُولَائِكَ الْمُعَلِّمُونَ

كَانُوا الْيَوْمَ فِي يَافَا ١١. أَخِي تَعَلَّمَ فِي الْمَدْرَسَةِ

اللُّغَةَ الْعَرَبِيَّةَ وَاللُّغَةَ الْإِنْكِلِيزِيَّةَ ١٢. أَيْنَ كَلْبُكَ

الْآنَ ؟- هُوَ الْآنَ فِي غُرْفَةِ الْجَدَّةِ ١٣. الْمُعَلِّمُونَ

وَالْمُعَلِّمَاتُ كَانُوا الْيَوْمَ فِي الْقُدْسِ ١٤. أَيْنَ مُعَلِّمَاتُ

هٰذِهِ الْمَدْرَسَةِ ؟- هُنَّ فِي كَرْمِ جَدَّتِي.

Vocabulary:

267. مُسْلِم "Moslem" 268. خَمْر "wine"

269. خِنْزِير "swine" 270. جَامِع "mosque" 271. حَارَة "quarter (of

a town") 272. تَعَلَّم "to learn" 273. لُغَة "language" 274. عَرَبِيّ

"Arabic"; "Arabian" (fem. عَرَبِيَّة) 275. شَارِع "street"

276. جِهَة 277. إِنْكِلِيزِيّ "English" (fem. إِنْكِلِيزِيَّة)

"side"; "direction" 278. أَرْبَع "four" 279. شَرْق "east" 280. غَرْب

"west" 281. شَمَال "north"; "left" and جَنُوب "south"

283. أَمَام "before"; "in front of" 284. صَاح "to shout"; "to cry out"

(Imperfect: أَصِيح) 285. صَوْت "voice" 286. عَال "high"; "loud

(voice)" 287. القُدْس "Jerusalem" 288. هَؤُلَاء "these" (masc and

fem.) 289. أُولَاكَ or أُولَائِكَ and also; أُولَالِكَ "those" (m. and f.).

Translate:

1. My son was to-day in the school which is in the Jaffa street 2. Our uncle (on the father's side) was to-day in Jerusalem and my teacher too was there 3. Where is now my small sister? — She plays in front of the mosque 4. This street is longer than that street 5. The bakers were to-day in the garden of the grand-father 6. Who saw the tailors to-day?— I saw the tailors in the after-noon 7. The teachers of this school were to-day in the vineyard of my brother 8. I learned the English language in this school 9. Where did thy (masc.) son learn the Arabic language? — He learned the Arabic language in Jaffa 10. The director and the teachers of this school (in Arabic: The director of this school and its teachers) have returned to-day from Jerusalem.

Thirty-ninth Lesson

اَلْجِهَاتُ ٱلْأَرْبَع

لَمَّا رَجَعَ أَحْمَدُ مِنَ ٱلْمَدْرَسَةِ سَأَلَتْهُ أُمُّهُ: مَا
تَعَلَّمْتَ فِي ٱلْمَدْرَسَةِ. فَقَالَ أَحْمَدُ تَعَلَّمْنَا ٱلْجِهَاتِ
ٱلْأَرْبَعَ. وَهِيَ ٱلشَّرْقُ وَٱلْغَرْبُ وَٱلشِّمَالُ وَٱلْجَنُوبُ.
وَقَدْ قَالَ لَنَا ٱلْمُعَلِّمُ إِنَّ ٱلْجِهَةَ ٱلَّتِي تُشْرِقُ مِنْهَا
ٱلشَّمْسُ هِيَ ٱلشَّرْقُ وَٱلْجِهَةُ ٱلَّتِي تَغِيبُ فِيهَا
ٱلشَّمْسُ هِيَ ٱلْغَرْبُ وَٱلَّتِي تَكُونُ عَلَى يَمِينِنَا
إِذَا قَابَلْنَا جِهَةَ ٱلشَّرْقِ هِيَ ٱلْجَنُوبُ وَٱلَّتِي تَكُونُ
عَلَى يَسَارِنَا هِيَ ٱلشِّمَالُ.

فَوَقَّفَتْهُ أُمُّهُ بِوَجْهِهِ إِلَى جِهَةِ ٱلْغَرْبِ وَقَالَتْ
لَهُ: سَمِّ لِي ٱلْآنَ ٱلْجِهَاتِ وَأَشِرْ عَلَيْهَا. فَقَالَ
أَحْمَدُ: ٱلْغَرْبُ أَمَامِي وَٱلشَّرْقُ خَلْفِي وَٱلشِّمَالُ عَلَى
يَمِينِي وَٱلْجَنُوبُ عَلَى يَسَارِي.

أَسْئِلَةٌ: لَمَّا رَجَعَ أَحْمَدُ مِنَ ٱلْمَدْرَسَةِ مَا سَأَلَتْهُ

أُمُّهُ؟ مَا أَجَابَ أَحْمَدُ؟ مَا قَالَ الْمُعَلِّمُ؟ كَيْفَ

وَقَفَتْهُ أُمُّهُ وَمَا قَالَتْ لَهُ؟ مَا قَالَ أَحْمَدُ؟

Vocabulary: 290. لَمَّا "when" 291. إِنَّ "indeed"; "verily";

"truly" (The sentence in Arabic is often introduced by the particle إِنَّ

which is followed by the subject in the accusative case e. g.

إِنَّ الْبَيْتَ

"(verily) the house is big" كَبِيرٌ) 292. إِنَّ "that" (only after

the verb قَالَ "to say" For example: قَالَ إِنَّ الْبَيْتَ كَبِيرٌ

"he said that the house is big ") 293. أَشْرَقَ "to shine"; "to rise"

(Imperfect: أَشْرِقُ) 294. شَمْسٌ "sun" 295. غَابَ "to be absent";

"to depart". 296. فِي "in" (فِيهَا "in her (it)" 297. يَمِينٌ "right

side" 298. يَسَارٌ "left side" 299. قَابَلَ "to be in front of"; "to be

opposite to" 300. وَقَفَ "to place"; "to cause to stand" 301. وَجْهٌ

"face" 302. سَمَّى "to name" (Imperative: سَمِّ) 303. أَشَارَ

"to indicate" (Imperative: أَشِرْ) 304. خَلْفٌ "back" 305. خَلْفَ

"behind" (prep.) ـ خَلْفِي behind me خَلْفَكَ، خَلْفُكِ، خَلْفَهُ etc.

Fourtieth Lesson

اَلصَّدَى

كَانَ زَيْدٌ يَوْمًا فِي اَلْغَابَةِ اَلْقَرِيبَةِ مِنَ اَلْمَدِينَةِ .

وَبَيْنَمَا كَانَ يَلْعَبُ هُنَاكَ صَاحَ بِصَوْتٍ عَالٍ: هَا هَا هَا .

فَسَمِعَ فِي اَلْحَالِ صَوْتًا آخَرَ فِي اَلْغَابَةِ يَـقُولُ:

هَا هَا هَا . فَظَنَّ زَيْدٌ أَنَّ فِي اَلْغَابَةِ وَلَدًا آخَرَ . لِأَنَّهُ

كَانَ لَا يَعْرِفُ مَا هُوَ اَلصَّدَى . فَقَالَ: مَنْ أَنْتَ يَا

هٰذَا؟ فَسَمِعَ حَالًا اَلصَّوْتَ اَلْآخَرَ يَقُولُ: مَنْ أَنْتَ

يَا هٰذَا؟ فَظَنَّ زَيْدٌ أَنَّ اَلْوَلَدَ اَلْآخَرَ يَهْزَأُ بِهِ فَقَالَ:

أَنْتَ جَاهِلٌ أَحْمَقُ .

فَقَالَ اَلصَّوْتُ اَلْآخَرُ: أَنْتَ جَاهِلٌ أَحْمَقُ .

فَغَضِبَ زَيْدٌ وَرَفَعَ صَوْتَهُ وَصَاحَ بِصَوْتٍ

عَالٍ: أَنْتَ جَاهِلٌ أَحْمَقُ .

وَبَيْنَمَا هُوَ يَصِيحُ فَإِذَا بِأَبِيهِ قَدْ جَاءَ وَقَالَ لَهُ:

إِنَّكَ يَا اُبْنِي لَا تَسْمَعُ إِلَّا صَدَى صَوْتِكَ . فَلَمَّا

تَبَيَّنَ لِزَيْدٍ أَمْرُ اَلصَّدَى خَجِلَ وَرَجَعَ إِلَى اَلْبَيْتِ .

أَسْئِلَةٌ : أَيْنَ كَانَ زَيْدٌ؟ مَا فَعَلَ هُنَاكَ؟ لَمَّا

صَاحَ هَا هَا هَا هَا مَا سَمِعَ؟ مَا ظَنَّ زَيْدٌ؟ مَا قَالَ

زَيْدٌ؟ مَا سَمِعَ بَعْدَهُ؟ لَمَّا ظَنَّ أَنَّ الْوَلَدَ يَهْزَأُ بِهِ

مَا قَالَ؟ مَا سَمِعَ بَعْدَهُ؟ مَا فَعَلَ بَعْدَ ذٰلِكَ؟ مَنْ

جَاءَ وَقْتَمَا كَانَ يَصِيحُ؟ مَا قَالَ لَهُ أَبُوهُ؟ لَمَّا تَبَيَّنَ

لِزَيْدٍ أَمْرُ الصَّدَى مَا قَالَ؟

Vocabulary: 306. صَدَّى "echo" (الصَّدَى "the echo")
307. مَدِينَةٌ "city"; 308. ("one day"; "once") يَوْمًا "day" يَوْمٌ
309. حَالًا and also : فِي الْحَالِ "immediately" 310. ظَنَّ "town"
"to think"; "to believe" 311. هَزَأَ بِ "to mock at"; "to deride"
312. أَحْمَقُ "stupid"; "foolish" 313. غَضِبَ "to be angry"; "to
become angry" 314. جَاءَ "to come" 315 إِلَّا "except"; "only"
316. تَبَيَّنَ "to become clear"; "to be elucidate" 317. أَمْرٌ "matter";
"affair" 318 خَجِلَ "to be ashamed of" 319. بَعْدَهُ "after him";
"after it".

Note : لِأَنَّ "because" — لِأَنِّي "because I" لِأَنَّكَ، لِأَنَّكِ.
لِأَنَّنَا، لِأَنَّهَا، لِأَنَّهُ etc.

إِنَّ (see above page 96, vocabulary) — إِنِّي، إِنَّكَ، إِنَّكِ، إِنَّهُ etc.

Fourty-first Lesson

A

"dogs"	كِلَابٌ	"a dog"	كَلْبٌ
"houses"	بُيُوتٌ	"a house"	بَيْتٌ
"books"	كُتُبٌ	"a book"	كِتَابٌ
"men"	رِجَالٌ	"a man"	رَجُلٌ
"schools"	مَدَارِسُ	"a school"	مَدْرَسَةٌ

In Arabic there are two kinds of plurals which are generally known as the **sound** (or : the **strong**) and the **broken** (or : the **weak**) plurals.

Sound plural is the plural which is formed by adding the termination ـُونَ to masculine nouns (see above page 90) and the termination ـَاتٌ to the feminine nouns (see above page 91. B).

Broken plural is the plural which is formed as follows :

1. By internal change such as كَلْبٌ "dog", plural : كِلَابٌ ; بَيْتٌ "house", plural: بُيُوتٌ etc.

2. By internal change and by the addition of a termination, such as فَارِسٌ "rider", plural : فُرْسَانٌ ; وَزِيرٌ "minister", plural : وُزَرَاءُ etc.

3. By internal change and by the addition of a prefix, such as سَبَبٌ "cause", plur. أَسْبَابٌ ; وَلَدٌ "child", plural : أَوْلَادٌ

4. By internal change and by the addition of a termination as well as of a prefix, such as سُؤَالٌ "question", plural: أَسْئِلَةٌ.

Note 1: Some nouns have two or more different forms of **broken plural**, such as بَحْرٌ "sea", plural: بُحُورٌ, بِحَارٌ, أَبْحُرٌ and أَبْحَارٌ.

Some nouns have both the **sound** and the **broken-plurals**, such as إِبْنٌ "son", plural: أَبْنَاءٌ and بَنُونٌ.

Note 2: The forms of the **broken plural** are fairly numerous and usually cause the students some difficulty, though by no means as serious as it might appear at first sight.

The best way is to learn the plural of each noun together with its singular.

B

"big houses"	بُيُوتٌ كَبِيرَةٌ (1)	بَيْتٌ كَبِيرٌ "a big house"
"big schools"	مَدَارِسُ كَبِيرَةٌ	مَدْرَسَةٌ "a school"
"big animals"	حَيَوَانَاتٌ كَبِيرَةٌ (2)	
"these houses"	هٰذِهِ الْبُيُوتُ	هٰذِهِ الْمَدْرَسَةُ "this school"
"these schools"	هٰذِهِ الْمَدَارِسُ	
"these animals"	هٰذِهِ الْحَيَوَانَاتُ	

أَيْنَ الْكُتُبُ الْجَدِيدَةُ ؟ — هِيَ عَلَى مَائِدَتِي

"Where are the new books? — they are on my table"

(1) The **broken-plurals** are treated as feminine singulars thus:

هٰذِهِ ٱلْبُيُوتُ كَبِيرَةٌ "these houses are big"

هٰذِهِ ٱلْكُتُبُ رَخِيصَةٌ. إِشْتَرَيْتُهَا فِي ٱلدُّكَّانِ "these books are cheap. I bought them in the shop"

Exceptions are the nouns which denote persons e. g.

هُؤُلَاءِ ٱلرِّجَالُ "these men" **and not:** هٰذِهِ ٱلرِّجَالُ ;

ٱلْأَوْلَادُ ٱلْمُجْتَهِدُونَ "the diligent pupils"

2) When the noun which does not denote persons is in the **sound-plural** it is also treated as a feminine singular e. g.

هٰذِهِ ٱلْحَيَوَانَاتُ كَبِيرَةٌ "these animals are big".

Fourty-second Lesson

١. أَيْنَ ٱلْجَرَائِدُ ٱلَّتِي ٱشْتَرَيْتُهَا قَبْلَ ٱلظُّهْرِ ؟ –

هِيَ عَلَى مَائِدَتِي   ٢. أَيْنَ ٱشْتَرَيْتَ هٰذِهِ ٱلدَّفَاتِرَ ٱلْجَدِيدَةَ ؟ – إِشْتَرَيْتُهَا فِي ٱلدُّكَّانِ ٱلْجَدِيدِ ٣. خُذْ هٰذَا ٱلطَّبَاشِيرَ وَأَرْسُمْ رَجُلًا عَلَى ٱللَّوْحِ   ٤. ٱللَّوْحُ أَسْوَدُ وَٱلطَّبَاشِيرُ أَبْيَضُ   ٥. سَفِينَةٌ وَاحِدَةٌ مِنَ ٱلسُّفُنِ ٱلَّتِي رَأَيْتُهَا فِي ٱلصَّبَاحِ قَدْ غَرِقَتْ بَعْدَ ٱلظُّهْرِ   ٦. ٱلدُّبُّ أَكْبَرُ مِنَ ٱلذِّئْبِ وَٱلْفِيلُ أَكْبَرُ

مِنَ الدُّبِّ.   7. رَأَيْتُ الْيَوْمَ تَلَامِيذَ هٰذِهِ الْمَدْرَسَةِ

فِي الْغَابَةِ الْقَرِيبَةِ مِنْ يَافَا   8. مَتَى اشْتَرَيْتَ هٰذِهِ

الْكُتُبَ ؟ - اِشْتَرَيْتُهَا فِي السَّنَةِ الْمَاضِيَةِ   9. بِكَمْ

بَاعَ الْفَلَّاحُ الثَّعْلَبَ وَ بِكَمِ اشْتَرَى الْحِمَارَ ؟ - اَلْفَلَّاحُ

بَاعَ الثَّعْلَبَ بِلِيرَةٍ فَلَسْطِينِيَّةٍ وَاشْتَرَى الْحِمَارَ بِلِيرَتَيْنِ

فَلَسْطِينِيَّتَيْنِ   10. هٰذَا التَّاجِرُ وَشَرِيكُهُ فَتَحَا دُكَّانًا

جَدِيدًا فِي السُّوقِ الْجَدِيدِ   11. شُرَكَاءُ هٰذِهِ الشَّرِكَةِ

أَغْنَى مِنْ شُرَكَاءِ تِلْكَ الشَّرِكَةِ   12. هٰذِهِ الْأَرَانِبُ

أَكْبَرُ مِنْ تِلْكَ الْأَرَانِبِ   13. اَلْبُيُوتُ فِي هٰذَا

الشَّارِعِ أَكْبَرُ مِنَ الْبُيُوتِ الَّتِي فِي ذٰلِكَ الشَّارِعِ

14. رَأَيْتُ الْيَوْمَ تَلَامِيذَ هٰذِهِ الْمَدْرَسَةِ فِي الْغَابَةِ

الْكَبِيرَةِ الْقَرِيبَةِ مِنْ حَيْفَا.

Vocabulary: 320. خُذْ imperative of أَخَذَ 321. طَبَاشِيرُ

"chalk" 322. رَجُلٌ "man" (plur. رِجَالٌ) 323. سَفِينَةٌ "ship" (plur.

سُفُنٌ) 324. غَرِقَ "to sink"; "to drown" (Imperf. أَغْرَقُ)

325. دُبٌّ "bear" (plur. أَدْبَابٌ) 326. ذِئْبٌ "wolf" (plur. ذِئَابٌ)

327. سَنَةٌ "year" (plur. سِنُونَ and also سَنَوَاتٌ) 328. اَلْمَاضِي

"the past" (fem. اَلْمَاضِيَةُ) 329. كَمْ "how many?"; "how much?"

330. بَاعَ "to sell" (Imperf. أَبِيعُ) 331. فَلَّاحٌ "peasant"; "farmer"

332. تَاجِرٌ "merchant" 333. لِيرَةٌ فَلَسْطِينِيَّةٌ "Palestinian pound"

334. شَرِيكٌ "companion"; "partner" (plur. شُرَكَاءُ) (تُجَّارٌ plur.)

335. شِرْكَةٌ and also: شَرِكَةٌ "company"; "partnership".

Fourty-third Lesson

١. زَرَعَ اَلْفَلَّاحُ اَلْيَوْمَ لِفْتًا فِي اَلْبُسْتَانِ ٢. صَاحِبُ
اَلْبَيْتِ كَانَ اَلْيَوْمَ فِي اَلْقَرْيَةِ وَأَشْتَرَى هُنَاكَ مِنَ
اَلْفَلَّاحِينَ تِبْنًا بِلِيرَةٍ فَلَسْطِينِيَّةٍ ٣. هٰؤُلَاءِ اَلتَّلَامِيذُ
مُجْتَهِدُونَ وَأُولَائِكَ اَلتَّلَامِيذُ كَسْلَانُونَ ٤. هٰذِهِ
اَلْمَدَارِسُ أَكْبَرُ مِنْ تِلْكَ اَلْمَدَارِسِ ٥. أَيْنَ تَرَكْتَ
كِلَابَ جَدِّي ؟- تَرَكْتُهَا فِي اَلْكَرْمِ ٦. هٰذِهِ
اَلْبُيُوتُ أَكْبَرُ مِنْ بُيُوتِ ذٰلِكَ اَلشَّارِعِ ٧. مَتَى
اُشْتَرَيْتَ هٰذِهِ اَلدُّيُوكَ ؟- إِشْتَرَيْتُهَا اَلْبَارِحَ ٨. مَا

رَسَمَ إِبْرَاهِيمُ فِي الدَّفْتَرِ الْجَدِيدِ ؟ – هُوَ رَسَمَ هُنَاكَ خُطُوطًا مُسْتَقِيمَةً ٩. هٰذَا الْخَطُّ أَطْوَلُ مِنْ كُلِّ الْخُطُوطِ الْأُخْرَى ١٠. بَنُوا الْجَارِ كَسْلَانُونَ وَ بَنَاتُهُ مُجْتَهِدَاتٌ ١١. بَنَاتُ أَخِي دَرَسْنَ فِي هٰذِهِ الْمَدْرَسَةِ وَ بَنُوهُ دَرَسُوا فِي الْمَدْرَسَةِ الَّتِي فِي الْمَدِينَةِ الْقَدِيمَةِ ١٢. أَلْفَلَّاحُونَ الَّذِينَ خَرَجُوا مِنَ الْجَامِعِ ذَهَبُوا إِلَى يَافَا ١٣. مِنْ أَيْنَ رَجَعَ التَّلَامِيذُ الَّذِينَ دَخَلُوا الْمَدْرَسَةَ الْآنَ ؟ – هُمْ رَجَعُوا مِنَ الْغَابَةِ ١٤. مَا أَعْطَى مُدِيرُ الْمَدْرَسَةِ التَّلَامِيذَ ؟ – هُوَ أَعْطَاهُمْ كُتُبًا جَدِيدَةً ١٥. هٰذِهِ الدَّفَاتِرُ غَالِيَةٌ. هِيَ أَغْلَى مِنْ تِلْكَ الدَّفَاتِرِ ١٦. أَلسُّكَّرُ الَّذِي اشْتَرَيْتُ فِي هٰذَا الدُّكَّانِ أَغْلَى مِنَ السُّكَّرِ الَّذِي اشْتَرَيْتُهُ فِي السُّوقِ.

Vocabulary: 336. زَرَعَ "to sow" (Imperfect: يَزْرَعُ)

337. لِفْتٌ "turnip"; 338. صَاحِبٌ "friend"; "owner"; "possessor"

339. قَرْيَةٌ "village" (plural: قُرًى "villages"; أَصْحَابٌ "plural")

كَسْلَان ("the villages") 340. تِبْن "straw" 341. مُجْتَهِد diligent 342.

"lazy" 343. الْبَارِحَة and also الْبَارِحَة "yesterday" 344. خَط "line"

(plur. خُطُوط) 345. مُسْتَقِيم "straight" 346. كُلّ followed by a

definite noun in plural is to be translated "all" e.g. كُلّ الْخُطُوط

"all the lines", كُلّ بُيُوتِهِ "all his houses" (see above p. 85 vocabulary)

إِبْنَة 348. "son" إِبْن is the plural of (أَبْنَاء and also) بَنُون 347.

and also بِنْت "daughter", "girl" (plur. بَنَات) 349. دَرَسَ

to study", "to learn" (imperf. يَدْرُس) 350. قَدِيم "old", "ancient"

351. الَّذِين "who" (relative pronoun, plur. masc.) 352. أَعْطَى "to give"

أَعْطَى التِّلْمِيذ "he gave to the pupil", أَعْطَاهُ "he gave him"

الْغَالِي (I gave") 353. غَالٍ "dear (price)"; "precious"

the dear", fem. غَالِيَة ; أَغْلَى مِنْ "more precious than").

Translate:

1. These farmers are richer than those farmers
2. Where did you (masd.) buy these new books ?— I bought them
n the new shop   3. These pupils are lazy and those pupils
re diligent   4. The possessor of these houses is rich. He is
richer than the pessessor of those houses   5. Where are the
ogs of the grand-father ? — they are (in Arabic she is) in the
arden of the neighbour 6. The pupils of this school have been
o-day in the forest and the pupils of that school were there
ester-day   7. The new house is bigger than the old house
My brother sold his old house and bought a new house

9. I saw yesterday a big bear in a cage   10. The schools in this village are small. They are (in Arabic : she is) smaller than the schools in that village   11. These copy-books are cheaper than those copy-books 12. These new houses are smaller than those old houses   13. These bakers are rich. They are richer than those bakers.

Forty-fourth Lesson

أَمْثَالٌ

رَأْسُ الْحِكْمَةِ مَخَافَةُ اللهِ

رَأْسُ الْكَسْلَانِ مَعْمَلُ الشَّيْطَانِ

مِنْ كَثْرَةِ الْمَلَّاحِينَ غَرِقَتِ السَّفِينَةُ

أَلْأَسْعَارُ وَالْأَعْمَارُ بِيَدِ اللهِ

رَاحَةُ الْجِسْمِ فِي قِلَّةِ الطَّعَامِ

وَرَاحَةُ اللِّسَانِ فِي قِلَّةِ الْكَلَامِ

هٰذَا الْحِمَارُ بِلِيرَةٍ وَسَرْجُهُ بِلِيرَتَيْنِ

أَلْقِطَارُ الَّذِي سَافَ

قَالَ الْمُعَلِّمُ لِأَحَدِ التَّلَامِيذِ ارْسُمْ عَلَى اللَّوْحِ طَارًا. فَتَقَرَّبَ التِّلْمِيذُ مِنَ اللَّوْحِ وَأَخَذَ الطَّبَاشِيرَ

بِيَدِهِ وَرَسَمَ عَلَى اللَّوْحِ خَطَّيْنِ مُسْتَقِيمَيْنِ وَمَا

رَسَمَ الْقِطَارَ.

الْمُعَلِّمُ: وَأَيْنَ الْقِطَارُ؟

التِّلْمِيذُ: قَدْ سَافَرَ بَا مُعَلِّمِي.

أَسْئِلَةٌ: مَا قَالَ الْمُعَلِّمُ لِتِلْمِيذِهِ؟ مَا رَسَمَ التِّلْمِيذُ؟

مَا سَأَلَ الْمُعَلِّمُ؟ مَا أَجَابَ التِّلْمِيذُ؟

Vocabulary: 354. قِطَارٌ "train"; "railway train" 355. سَافَرَ

"to travel"; "to make a journey" 356. رَأْسٌ "head"; "beginning"

plural: (رُؤُوسٌ) 357. حِكْمَةٌ "wisdom" 358. مَخَافَةٌ "fear";

359. أَللهُ "God"; "Allah" 360. كَثْرَةٌ "abundance"; "multiplicity"

361. عُمْرٌ "current price"; "rate" (plural, أَسْعَارٌ) 362. سِعْرٌ

"age"; "life-time" (plural, أَعْمَارٌ) 363. رَاحَةٌ "rest"; "comfort";

"ease" 364. جِسْمٌ "body" 365. قِلَّةٌ "littleness"; "smallness";

366. طَعَامٌ "food", "nourishment" 367. كَلَامٌ "speech", "talk"

368. سَرْجٌ "saddle" (plur. سُرُوجٌ).

Forty-fifth Lesson

أَلشَّرِيكَانِ

شَارَكَ دُبٌّ فَلَّاحًا فِي زِرَاعَةٍ وَاتَّفَقَا فِي أَلسَّنَةِ الْأُولَى أَنْ يَأْخُذَ أَلْفَلَّاحُ مَا يَنْبُتُ تَحْتَ أَلتُّرْبَةِ وَالدُّبُّ مَا فَوْقَهَا

فَزَرَعَا لِفْتًا. وَلَمَّا حَانَ وَقْتُ أَلتَّقْسِيمِ أَخَذَ أَلْفَلَّاحُ رُؤُوسَ أَللِّفْتِ وَأَعْطَى أَلدُّبَّ أَلْأَوْرَاقَ.

لَمَّا رَأَى أَلدُّبُّ أَنَّهُ مَخْدُوعٌ بِهٰذَا أَلشَّرْطِ طَلَبَ أَنْ تَكُونَ حِصَّتُهُ فِي أَلسَّنَةِ أَلتَّالِيَةِ مَا تَحْتَ أَلتُّرْبَةِ وَحِصَّةُ شَرِيكِهِ مَا فَوْقَهَا .

فَوَافَقَهُ أَلْفَلَّاحُ بِذٰلِكَ وَزَرَعَا أَلْأَرْضَ قَمْحًا. وَلَمَّا حَانَ وَقْتُ أَلتَّقْسِيمِ أَخَذَ أَلْفَلَّاحُ أَلسَّنَابِلَ وَالتِّبْنَ وَتَرَكَ لِلدُّبِّ أَلْجُذُورَ أَلَّتِي لَا قِيمَةَ لَهَا . فَرَأَى أَلدُّبُّ أَنَّهُ مَخْدُوعٌ فِي كُلِّ حَالٍ. فَتَرَكَ أَلشَّرِكَةَ.

<u>Vocabulary:</u> 369. شَارَكَ "to enter into partnership with"

370. زَرْعٌ "sowing", "planting" 371. حَقْلٌ "field" 372. إتَّفَقَ فِي

(يَنْبُتُ) .Imperf) "to sprout"• ,"to grow" نَبَتَ .to agree upon" 373"

374. لَمَّا "when the time of... came" ... تُرْبَةٌ "soil", "ground" 375. فَوْقَ "above", "on" 376

377. تَقْسِيمٌ "division" ... حَانَ ٱلْوَقْتُ

378. وَرَقٌ "leaf" (plural : أَوْرَاقٌ) 379. مَخْدُوعٌ "deceived"

380. شَرْطٌ "condition" (plural : شُرُوطٌ) 381. طَلَبَ "to ask for",

"to wish for"; "to desire" (Imperfect يَطْلُبُ) 382. حِصَّةٌ "share",

"portion" 383. أَلتَّالِي "the following"; "the next" (fem. أَلتَّالِيَةُ)

384. وَافَقَ "to agree to" 385. قَمْحٌ "wheat" 386. سُنْبُلَةٌ "ear of

corn" (plural : سَنَابِلُ) 387. جِذْرٌ "root" (plural : جُذُورٌ)

388. قِيمَةٌ "value"; "worth"; price" 389 حَالٌ "state"; "condition"

Forty-sixth Lesson

"Salim is poor" سَلِيمٌ فَقِيرٌ	"Ahmad is poor" أَحْمَدُ فَقِيرٌ
"the house of Salim" بَيْتُ سَلِيمٍ	"the house of Ahmad" (1) بَيْتُ أَحْمَدَ
"I saw Salim" رَأَيْتُ سَلِيمًا	"I saw Ahmad" رَأَيْتُ أَحْمَدَ
"in the books" فِي ٱلْكُتُبِ	"in the schools" (2) فِي ٱلْمَدَارِسِ

(1) There are nouns and adjectives with no **Tanwin** at the end

e. g. أَحْمَدُ ;Ahmad" كَسْلَانُ "lazy" ;أَسْوَدُ "black" ;مَدَارِسُ

دَفَاتِرُ "copy-books" ;"schools" etc.

These **Tanwin-less** nouns and adjectives have two case-endings only :

a. ٗ (u) in the Nominative e. g. أَحْمَدُ فِي الْبُسْتَانِ "Ahmad

is in the garden".

b. ِ (a) in both the Genitive and the Accusative e. g. بَيْتُ

أَحْمَدَ "the house of Ahmad" ; فِي مَدَارِسَ جَدِيدَةٍ

"in new schools" ; فِي بَيْتٍ أَبْيَضَ "in a white house" ;

رَأَيْتُ أَحْمَدَ "I saw Ahmad" ; رَأَيْتُ مَدَارِسَ جَدِيدَةً

رَأَيْتُ بَيْتًا أَبْيَضَ "I saw a white house

(2) When the **Tanwin-less** nouns and adjectives are made definite by the Article أَلْ or by a possessive suffix or by a following Genitive, then they have three case-endings e. g.

a. هٰذِهِ الْمَدَارِسُ جَدِيدَةٌ "these schools are new".

b. مُعَلِّمُوا الْمَدَارِسِ "the teachers of the schools"

فِي مَدَارِسِ الْمَدِينَةِ "in the schools of the city"

فِي دَفَاتِرِهَا "in her copy-books"

c. رَأَيْتُ الْمَدَارِسَ "I saw the schools".

1. مَا عَلَى الْمَائِدَةِ ؟ – عَلَى الْمَائِدَةِ كُتُبٌ وَدَفَاتِرُ

وَجَرَائِدُ 2. نَحْنُ شَرِبْنَا قَهْوَةً فِي فَنَاجِينَ كَبِيرَةٍ

وَكُمْ شَرِبُوا قَهْوَةً فِي فَنَاجِينَ صَغِيرَةٍ ٣. مَا

اُشْتَرَيْتَ فِي الدُّكَّانِ الْجَدِيدِ ؟- إِشْتَرَيْتُ هُنَاكَ

جَرَائِدَ وَدَفَاتِرَ وَكُتُبًا ٤. قَدْ دَخَلَ سَارِقٌ غُرْفَةَ

أَخِي الْكَبِيرِ وَسَرَقَ السَّاعَةَ الَّتِي اشْتَرَاهَا أَخِي

الْبَارِحَ ٥. كَتَبْتُ الْيَوْمَ بِحِبْرٍ أَزْرَقَ وَأَخْتِي

كَتَبَتْ بِحِبْرٍ أَحْمَرَ ٦. كَانَ أَخِي فِي مَحْكَمَةِ

الصُّلْحِ وَرَأَى هُنَاكَ الْمُحَامِي الَّذِي كَانَ الْبَارِحَ

فِي كَرْمِ جَدِّي ٧. مَنْ رَأَى بَيْتِي الْجَدِيدَ ؟- أُمِّي

رَأَتْهُ الْبَارِحَ ٨. قَالَ أَبُوكَ إِنَّهُ يَنْتَظِرُكَ فِي

مَحْكَمَةِ الصُّلْحِ ٩. إِنْتَظَرَكَ الْخَيَّاطُ قَبْلَ الظُّهْرِ

فِي دُكَّانِهِ الَّذِي فِي حَارَةِ الْمُسْلِمِينَ ١٠. أَيْنَ الْجُبْنَةُ

الَّتِي اشْتَرَيْتُهَا فِي السُّوقِ ؟- هِيَ فِي الْمَطْبَخِ

١١. إِشْتَرَيْتُ الْيَوْمَ فِي السُّوقِ تُفَّاحًا وَعِنَبًا وَجَوْزًا

١٢. هٰذِهِ التُّفَّاحَةُ حَامِضَةٌ وَتِلْكَ التُّفَّاحَةُ حُلْوَةٌ

١٣. هٰذِهِ الْجَوْزَةُ أَكْبَرُ مِنْ تِلْكَ الْجَوْزَةِ

Vocabulary: 390. سَارِق "thief" 391. سَرَقَ "to steal"

(Imperfect: يَسْرِقُ) 392. سَاعَة "hour" and also: "watch";

(مَحَاكِم "clock" 393. مَحْكَمَة "court of justice" (plural:

394. صُلْح "peace", "reconciliation" 395. مُحَامٍ "advocate",

"barrister" (الْمُحَامِي "the advocate") 396. رَأَتْ "she saw"

(رَأَتْهُ she saw him (it)) 397. إِنْتَظَرَ "to expect", "to wait for"

(Imperf.: يَنْتَظِرُ) 398. جُبْنَة "a piece of cheese" (see below Note)

399. مَطْبَخ "kitchen" 400. تُفَّاح "apples" 401. عِنَب "grapes"

402. حَامِض "sour" 403. حُلْو "sweet".

Note : Many nouns which denote plants or materials
have two singular forms :

1. A form without ة in the end. This form denotes the plant
   or the material generally. For example :

   الْتُفَّاحُ فَاكِهَةٌ "the apple is a fruit",

   جُبْنٌ يُصْنَعُ مِنْ حَلِيبٍ "cheese is produced from milk".

   The nouns in this singular form are to be translated
   sometimes as if they were plurals e. g.

   إِشْتَرَيْتُ فِي الْسُّوقِ تُفَّاحًا وَعِنَبًا وَجَوْزًا "I bought

   in the market apples, grapes and nuts".

2. A form with ة in the end. This form indicates a single object

of the named plant or a piece of the named material e. g.

لِي تُفَّاحَةٌ وَلَهُ تُفَّاحَةٌ "I have an apple and he has
an apple",

هَذِهِ الْجُبْنَةُ أَكْبَرُ مِنْ تِلْكَ الْجُبْنَةِ "this piece
of cheese is bigger than that piece of cheese".

"Two apples", "two pieces of cheese" is to be translated :

تُفَّاحَتَانِ ، جُبْنَتَانِ.

Translate: 1. This clock is bigger than the clock which thy (masc.) brother bought in Jerusalem   2. Where is the (piece of) cheese which I put on the table? — It is on the table in the kitchen   3. This apple is sour. It is sourer than that apple 4. Who has seen to-day the director of this school? — I have seen him to-day   5. This new house is smaller than the old house of the uncle (on the father's side)   6. What did thy (masc) brother buy in the new shop? — He bought there books and copy-books   7. The houses in this village are bigger than the houses of that village   8. I have a white dog and a black dog. The white dog is fatter than the black dog. 9. Who has seen Ahmad to-day? — My mother has seen him in the new market   10. Ibrahīm is bigger than Ahmad and Ahmad is bigger than Salīm   11. My father was yersterday in the field of Ibrahīm.

Forty-seventh Lesson

أَلْبَبْغَاءُ

كَانَ لِرَجُلٍ بَبْغَاءُ جَمِيلَةٌ تَعْرِفُ الْكَلَامَ وَإِذَا
مَرَّ بِهَا رَجُلٌ قَالَتْ لَهُ «نَهَارُكَ سَعِيدٌ يَا أَخِى» وَكَانَتْ
تَخْرُجُ إِلَى الْبُسْتَانِ بَعْدَ الظُّهْرِ وَتَنْتَظِرُ صَاحِبَهَا إِلَى
أَنْ رَجَعَ مِنْ دُكَّانِهِ. وَلَمَّا رَأَتْهُ كَانَتْ تَقُولُ: يَا

عَمِّي خُذْنِي إِلَى الْبَيْتِ . فَضَاعَتِ الْبَبْغَاءُ يَوْمًا .

فَكَانَ صَاحِبُهَا يَسْأَلُ كُلَّ النَّاسِ عَنْهَا فَقَالَ لَهُ أَحَدُ

الرِّجَالِ: إِنِّي سَمِعْتُ صَوْتَ بَبْغَاءَ فِي بَيْتِ جَارِي .

فَذَهَبَ صَاحِبُ الْبَبْغَاءِ إِلَى جَارِ ذَلِكَ الرَّجُلِ

وَسَأَلَهُ عَنِ الْبَبْغَاءِ . فَلَمَّا سَمِعَتْ صَوْتَ صَاحِبِهَا

قَالَتْ «يَا عَمِّي خُذْنِي إِلَى الْبَيْتِ» . فَدَخَلَ الرَّجُلُ

وَأَخَذَهَا مِنْ بَيْتِ السَّارِقِ .

أَسْئِلَةٌ : مَا كَانَتِ الْبَبْغَاءُ تَقُولُ لِكُلِّ وَاحِدٍ إِذَا

كَانَ يَمُرُّ بِهَا؟ لِمَاذَا كَانَتْ تَخْرُجُ إِلَى الْبُسْتَانِ؟ لَمَّا

رَأَتْ صَاحِبَهَا يَرْجِعُ مِنْ دُكَّانِهِ مَا قَالَتْ لَهُ؟ لَمَّا

ضَاعَتِ الْبَبْغَاءُ مَا فَعَلَ صَاحِبُهَا؟ مَا قَالَ لَهُ أَحَدُ الرِّجَالِ؟

Vocabulary: 404. بَبْغَاءِ "parrot", "popinjay" 405. مَرَّ
"to pass" (مَرَّ بِالْبَيْتِ "he passed the house" ,مَرَّ بِي ,مَرَّ بِكَ
etc.) 406. نَهَارٌ "day", "daytime" 407. سَعِيدٌ "fortunate", "lucky"
408. ضَاعَ "to be lost" 409. نَاسٌ is plural of إِنْسَانٌ
410. عَنْ "for", "about", "from".

Forty-eighth Lesson

A

"thy (masc.) house"	بَيْتُكَ (1)	بَيْتٌ
"thy (masc.) school"	مَدْرَسَتُكَ (2)	مَدْرَسَةٌ
"thy (masc.) two houses"	بَيْتَاكَ (3)	بَيْتَانِ
"in thy (masc.) two houses"	فِي بَيْتَيْكَ	فِي بَيْتَيْنِ
"thy (masc.) teachers"	مُعَلِّمُوكَ	مُعَلِّمُونَ
"with thy (masc.) teachers"	مَعَ مُعَلِّمِيكَ	مَعَ مُعَلِّمِينَ
"his (female) teachers"	مُعَلِّمَاتُهُ	مُعَلِّمَاتٌ
"thy (masc.) houses"	بُيُوتُكَ	بُيُوتٌ
"thy (masc.) big house" (4)	بَيْتُكَ الْـكَبِيرُ	بَيْتٌ كَبِيرٌ

(1) A personal suffix added to a noun denotes the property of the noun to the person which the pronominal suffix refered to. e.g. بَيْتُهُ "his house"; بَيْتُهَا "her house". These personal suffixes are therefore called **Possessive Pronouns**.
A possessive pronoun added to a noun defines it completely just as the article أَلْ would do, for "his house" specifies a definite (particular) house. The nouns drop therefore the **Tanwîn** (see above Lesson 23(3)) before the possessive pronouns e.g.

بَيْتُهُ "his house" (بَيْتٌ "a house")

(2) Feminine nouns ending in ة change this termination into ت

before the possessive pronouns e.g. مَدْرَسَتُكَ "thy (masc.)

school· (مَدْرَسَة· "a school")

(3) Nouns to which the possessive pronouns are attached take
the forms which they have before a genitive e.g.

the بَيْتَا الْخَبَّازِ "thy (masc.) two houses" (and also: بَيْتَاكَ

two houses of the baker". See above Lesson 32 C. (1))

فِي بَيْتَيْ "in thy (masc.) two houses· (so also: فِي بَيْتَيْكَ

"in the two houses of Salīm". See above)

رَأَيْتُ بَيْتَيْكَ "I saw thy (masc.) two houses· (so also:

رَأَيْتُ بَيْتَيْ سَلِيمٍ "I saw the two houses of Salīm")

مُعَلِّمُوا سَلِيمٍ "thy (masc.) teachers· (so also: مُعَلِّمُوكَ

"the teachers of Salīm". See above Lesson 37A.(3))

رَأَيْتُ "I saw thy (masc.) teachers" (so also: رَأَيْتُ مُعَلِّمِيكَ

مُعَلِّمِي سَلِيمٍ "I saw the teachers of Salīm". See above)

بَيْتُكَ "thy (masc.) house· (so also: بَيْتُ سَلِيمٍ "the house

of Salīm". See above Lesson 25 (1)b. Note)

فِي بَيْتِ سَلِيمٍ "in thy (masc.) house· (so also: فِي بَيْتِكَ

"in the house of Salīm".)

(4) When an adjective is added to a noun which has a possessive
pronoun it is necessary to make the adjective definite e. g.

بَيْتُكَ الْكَبِيرُ "thy (masc.) big house",

بَيْتَاكَ الْكَبِيرَانِ "thy (masc.) two big houses·

B

...ouns added by the possessive pronouns are as follows :

في بَ...	مُعَلِّمُونَ	بَيْتَانِ	فِي بَيْتٍ	بَيْتٌ	The person of the possessor	The number of the possessor
two ...uses	teachers	two houses	in a house	a house		
في بَ...	مُعَلِّمُويَ	بَيْتَايَ (1)	فِي بَيْتِي	بَيْتِي	1 m.f.	Singular
في بَيْ...	مُعَلِّمُوكَ	بَيْتَاكَ	فِي بَيْتِكَ	بَيْتُكَ	2 m.	
في بَيْ...	مُعَلِّمُوكِ	بَيْتَاكِ	فِي بَيْتِكِ	بَيْتُكِ	2 f.	
في بَ...	مُعَلِّمُوهُ	بَيْتَاهُ (2)	فِي بَيْتِهِ	بَيْتُهُ	3 m.	
في بَ...	مُعَلِّمُوهَا	بَيْتَاهَا	فِي بَيْتِهَا	بَيْتُهَا	3 f.	
					1 m.f.	Dual
في بَيْتَي...	مُعَلِّمُوكُمَا	بَيْتَا كُمَا	فِي بَيْتِكُمَا	بَيْتُكُمَا	2 m.f.	
في بَيْ...	مُعَلِّمُوهُمَا	بَيْتَاهُمَا	فِي بَيْتِهِمَا	بَيْتُهُمَا	3 m.f.	
في بَ...	مُعَلِّمُونَا	بَيْتَانَا	فِي بَيْتِنَا	بَيْتُنَا	1 m.f.	Plural
في بَيْتِي...	مُعَلِّمُوكُمْ	بَيْتَاكُمْ	فِي بَيْتِكُمْ	بَيْتُكُمْ	2 m.	
في بَيْتِي...	مُعَلِّمُوكُنَّ	بَيْتَاكُنَّ	فِي بَيْتِكُنَّ	بَيْتُكُنَّ	2 f.	
في بَيْتِ...	مُعَلِّمُوهُمْ	بَيْتَاهُمْ	فِي بَيْتِهِمْ	بَيْتُهُمْ	3 m.	
في بَيْتِ...	مُعَلِّمُوهُنَّ	بَيْتَاهُنَّ	فِي بَيْتِهِنَّ	بَيْتُهُنَّ	3 f.	

For the first person there is no special Dual form.

(1) The pronominal suffix of the first person is ي when it

follows a vowelless ي و ا For example :

بَيْتَايَ "my two houses"; مُعَلِّمُويَ "my teachers"

Note: فِي بَيْتَيَّ "in my two houses" instead of فِي بَيْتَيَّ :

رَأَى مُعَلِّمِيَّ "he saw my teachers" instead of رَأَى مُعَلِّمِيَّ

(2) The suffixes ه .هُمَا .هُمْ .هُنَّ .ه .هِمَا are changed into

هِمْ .هِنَّ when they follow the vowel ـِ (i), the ي (î) or

the يْ (ay) e. g. فِي بَيْتِهِ "in his house" ؛

فِي بَيْتِهِمْ "in their (masc.) house"; فِي بَيْتَيْهِ "in his two houses";

رَأَيْتُ مُعَلِّمِيهِ "I saw his teachers" etc.

Note : The prepositions also take the pronominal suffixes
as follows .

لِ "to", "for" ـِ لِي "to me" or "I have" لَكَ .لَكِ .لَهُ .لَهَا etc.

بِ "with"; "in" ـِ بِي .بِكَ .بِكِ .بِهِ .بِهَا etc.

إِلَى "to", "into" ـِ إِلَيَّ .إِلَيْكَ .إِلَيْكِ .إِلَيْهِ .إِلَيْهَا etc.

عَلَى "on" ـِ عَلَيَّ .عَلَيْكَ .عَلَيْكِ .عَلَيْهِ .عَلَيْهَا etc.

قَبْلَ "before" ـِ قَبْلِي .قَبْلَكَ .قَبْلَكِ .قَبْلَهُ .قَبْلَهَا etc.

مِنْ "from", "of", "than" ـِ مِنِّى .مِنْكَ .مِنْكِ .مِنْهُ etc.

Forty-ninth Lesson

١. أَبُو أَبِي وَأَبُو أُمِّي هُمَا جَدَّايَ. أُمُّ أَبِي وَأُمُّ أُمِّي هُمَا جَدَّتَايَ وَأَنَا حَفِيدُهُمْ ٢. مَا غَرَسَ جَدُّكَ ٱلْيَوْمَ فِي بُسْتَانِكُمْ ؟ – جَدِّي غَرَسَ ٱلْيَوْمَ نَخْلًا فِي بُسْتَانِنَا ٣. سَلِيمٌ وَوَالِدُهُ خَرَجَا مِنْ مَحْكَمَةِ ٱلصُّلْحِ وَرَجَعَا إِلَى بَيْتِهِمَا ٱلَّذِي فِي ٱلْمَدِينَةِ ٱلْقَدِيمَةِ ٤. سَلْمَى وَوَالِدَتُهَا كَانَتَا ٱلْيَوْمَ فِي ٱلْجَامِعِ ٥. أَبِي وَأُمِّي هُمَا وَالِدَايَ وَأَنَا ٱبْنُهُمَا. لِوَالِدَيَّ أَبْنَاءٌ وَبَنَاتٌ غَيْرِي. فَـأَبْنَاؤُهُمْ إِخْوَتِي وَبَنَاتُهُمْ أَخَوَاتِي ٦. كَانَ أَخِي فِي ٱلْقُدْسِ مَرَّةً وَفِي حَيْـفَا مَرَّتَيْنِ ٧. أُخْتِي كَانَتِ ٱلْيَوْمَ فِي حَدِيقَةِ ٱلْحَـيَـوَانَاتِ وَرَأَتْ هُنَاكَ نُسُورًا مُخْتَلِفَةً ٨. مَا هُوَ ٱلشَّيْءُ ٱلَّذِي حَمَلَهُ ٱلشَّيْخُ مِنَ ٱلْغَابَةِ ؟ – ٱلشَّيْخُ حَمَلَ حُزْمَةَ حَطَبٍ مِنْ هُنَاكَ ٩. أَيْنَ ٱلْكُتُبُ ٱلْجَدِيدَةُ ٱلَّـتِي ٱشْتَرَيْتِهَا ٱلْبَارِحَ ؟ – أَخَذَهَا أَخِي ٱلْـكَـبِـيـرُ ١٠. مُعَلِّمُويَ وَمُعَلِّمُوكَ كَانُوا ٱلْيَوْمَ فِي حَارَةِ ٱلْمُسْلِمِينَ ١١. بَنَاتُ جَارِنَا وَبَنُوهُ كَانُوا ٱلْيَوْمَ فِي ٱلْغَابَةِ ٱلْقَرِيبَةِ

12. مِنْ قَرْيَتِنَا. أَيْنَ كِتَابَاكَ الْجَدِيدَانِ وَأَيْنَ دَفْتَرَايَ؟ ـ كِتَابَايَ الْجَدِيدَانِ فِي غُرْفَتِي وَدَفْتَرَاكَ أَيْضًا هُنَاكَ.

Vocabulary:

411. حَفِيدٌ "grandson" (plural : أَحْفَادٌ)

412. غَرَسَ "to plant trees" 413. نَخْلٌ "date palms" 414. وَالِدٌ

"father" 415. وَالِدَةٌ "mother" 416. أَلْوَالِدَانِ "the parents" 417. أَخٌ

"brother" (plural: إِخْوَةٌ and إِخْوَانٌ) 418. أُخْتٌ "sister" (plural:

أَخَوَاتٌ) 419. مَرَّةٌ "once" ثَلَاثُ مَرَّاتٍ "three times" مِرَارًا

"often"; "several times") 420. نَسْرٌ "vulture"; "eagle" (plural: نُسُورٌ)

421. مُخْتَلِفٌ "different"; various" 422. شَيْءٌ "thing"; "something"

(plural: أَشْيَاءُ) 423. حَمَلَ "to carry"; to bear" (Imperf: يَحْمِلُ)

424. شَيْخٌ "an old man"; "chief"; "sheikh" (plural : شُيُوخٌ)

425. حَطَبٌ "package"; "bundle" 426. حُزْمَةٌ "fire-wood".

Fiftieth Lesson

1. كَمْ مَرَّةً كَانَ أَخُوكَ الْكَبِيرُ الْيَوْمَ فِي يَافَا؟ ـ أَخِي الْكَبِيرُ كَانَ الْيَوْمَ مَرَّتَيْنِ هُنَاكَ 2. هٰذَا

اَلصَّيَّادُ صَادَ ٱلْيَوْمَ أَرْنَبَيْنِ فَذَبَحَ أَحَدَهُمَا وَبَاعَ لَحْمَـهُ

فِي ٱلسُّوقِ. 3. هٰذَا ٱلصَّيَّادُ يَصِيدُ دَائِمًا فِي ٱلْغَابَةِ

ٱلْقَرِيبَةِ مِنْ قَرْيَتِكُمْ. 4. لِمَاذَا يَبْكِي ٱلْوَلَدُ وَٱلدُّمُوعُ

تَسِيلُ مِنْ عَيْنَيْهِ؟ ‑ هُوَ يَبْكِي مِنْ شِدَّةِ ٱلْبَرْدِ. 5. قَدْ

جَاءَ إِلَيَّ تِلْمِيذُكَ وَبَعْدَ مَا سَلَّمَ عَلَيَّ قَالَ إِنَّكَ تَنْتَظِرُنِي

فِي بَيْتِكَ ٱلْجَدِيدِ. 6. مُعَلِّمُ زَيْدٍ مَرَّ بِأَبِي وَسَلَّمَ عَلَيْهِ.

7. عَمُّكَ زَارَنِي ٱلْبَارِحَ وَأَنَا أَزُورُهُ غَدًا إِنْ شَاءَ ٱللهُ.

8. مَتَى يَزُورُنِي خَالُكَ؟ ‑ هُوَ يَزُورُكَ بَعْدَ ٱلظُّهْرِ

إِنْ شَاءَ ٱللهُ. 9. مُعَلِّمُوكَ زَارُوا ٱلْيَوْمَ مُعَلِّمِيَّ فِي

ٱلْمَدْرَسَةِ. 10. بُيُوتُكَ ٱلْجَدِيدَةُ أَكْبَرُ مِنْ بُيُوتِهِمُ

ٱلْجَدِيدَةِ. 11. مَنْ رَأَى بَيْتَيَّ ٱلْجَدِيدَيْنِ؟ ‑ أَنَا

رَأَيْتُهُمَا. 12. كَلْبَا أَخِي أَكْبَرُ مِنْ كَلْبَيْكَ.

Vocabulary: 427. كَمْ "how many ?", "how much ?"

(The noun after كَمْ is in the Accusative singular e. g, كَمْ بَيْتًا "how

many houses ?" كَمْ مَرَّةٌ "how many times ?") 428. صَيَّادٌ "hunter"

429. صَادَ "to hunt" (Imperfect: يَصِيدُ) 430. ذَبَحَ "to slaughter"

"to weep" بَكَى 431. دَائِمًا "always" 432. (Imperfect: يَذْبَحُ)

433. دَمْعٌ "tear" (plural: دُمُوعٌ) 434. سَالَ (Imperfect: يَبْكِي)

435. عَيْنٌ "eye" 436. سِيلُ (Imperfect: يَسِيلُ) "to flow", "to run" شِدَّةٌ

437. بَرْدٌ "cold", "coolness" 438. سَلَّمَ عَلَى "strength", "hardness"

439. زَارَ "to visit" (Imperfect: يَزُورُ) "to salute", "to greet"

440. إِنْ "if" 441. شَاءَ "to will", "to wish", "to desire"

(إِنْ شَاءَ ٱللهُ "God willing!").

Translate: 1. His two new books are in my small room
2. Where are our two dogs? — they are in the room of our
grand-father   3. How many books did thy father buy yesterday in the new shop?— My father bought yesterday two books
4. How many hares did the hunter hunt yesterday in this forest ?
—he hunted yesterday two hares   5. His brother visited me
yesterday and I shall visit him in the after-noon   6. Where
are my two copy-books ? — Thy (masc.) brother has taken them
7. Who has seen to-day the two asses of my grand-father?
—The brother of our neighbour saw them   8. The teachers of
the new school have to-day visited our teachers   9. These two
cows are fatter than our two cows   10. Our two horses are
bigger than your (masc.) two horses   11. How many copy-
books has thy (masc.) brother bought in the after-noon ? — He
has bought two copy-books   12. Our sister is bigger than your
(masc.) sister and your sister is bigger than his sister.

Fifty-first Lesson

صَيَّادٌ وَعُصْفُورٌ

كَانَ صَيَّادٌ يَصِيدُ عَصَافِيرَ فِي يَوْمٍ بَارِدٍ. فَكَانَ
يَذْبَحُهَا وَٱلدُّمُوعُ تَسِيلُ مِنْ عَيْنَيْهِ مِنْ شِدَّةِ ٱلْبَرْدِ.

فَقَالَ أَحَدُ الْعَصَافِيرِ لِصَاحِبِهِ: لَا تَخَفْ مِنْ هٰذَا الرَّجُلِ. أَلَا تَرَاهُ يَبْكِي؟ – فَقَالَ لَهُ آخَرُ. لَا تَنْظُرْ إِلَى دُمُوعِهِ بَلْ إِلَى مَا تَصْنَعُ يَدَاهُ.

أَرَانِبُ وَثَعَالِبُ

الْنُّسُورُ مَرَّةً وَقَعَتْ بَيْنَهُمْ وَبَيْنَ الْأَرَانِبِ حَرْبٌ. فَذَهَبَتِ الْأَرَانِبُ إِلَى الثَّعَالِبِ وَطَلَبُوا مِنْهُمْ أَنْ يُسَاعِدُوهُمْ فِي مُحَارَبَةِ النُّسُورِ. فَقَالُوا لَهُمْ: لَوْلَا عَرَفْنَاكُمْ وَلَوْلَا عَرَفْنَا النُّسُورَ الَّذِينَ تُحَارِبُونَهُمْ لَفَعَلْنَا ذٰلِكَ.

Vocabulary: 442. بَارِدٌ "cold", "cool" 443. لَا تَخَفْ "do not fear!" 444. أَلَا يَرَاهُ "does he not see him?" 445. نَظَرَ "to see", "to look" (لَا تَنْظُرْ "do not look!") 446. بَلْ "but" 447. وَقَعَ "to fall" 448. صَنَعَ "to make" (Imperfect: يَصْنَعُ) "to happen" 449. حَرْبٌ "war", "battle" 450. سَاعَدَ "to help", "to assist" (Imperfect: يُسَاعِدُ) 451. مَعْرَكَةٌ "battle,", "fight" 452. لَوْ "if" 453. لَوْلَا "if not" (حَارَبَ "to fight with")

454. لَ is a particle used for emphasis and it is omitted in translation e. g. لَفَعَلْنَا "(truly) we have done it". (Imperfect : يُحَارِبُ)

Fifty-second Lesson

"a big dog"	كَلْبٌ كَبِيرٌ
"a fat cow"	بَقَرَةٌ سَمِينَةٌ
"his dog is bigger than my dog"(1)	كَلْبُهُ أَكْبَرُ مِنْ كَلْبِي
"his cow is fatter than her cow"	بَقَرَتُهُ أَسْمَنُ مِنْ بَقَرَتِهَا
"he is the biggest in this village" (2)	هُوَ الْأَكْبَرُ فِي هٰذِهِ الْقَرْيَةِ
"she is the biggest in this village"	هِيَ الْكُبْرَى فِي هٰذِهِ الْقَرْيَةِ
"a red dog" (3)	كَلْبٌ أَحْمَرُ
"a red cow"	بَقَرَةٌ حَمْرَاءُ
"dumb children"	أَوْلَادٌ خُرْسٌ

(1) The comparative degree of the adjectives is always formed on the pattern of أَكْبَرُ thus:

أَسْمَنُ مِنْ "fatter than" — "fat" سَمِينٌ

أَصْغَرُ مِنْ "smaller than" — "small" صَغِيرٌ

أَطْوَلُ مِنْ "longer than" — "long" طَوِيلٌ etc.

The comparative form is the same for all genders and numbers e. g.

كَلْبِي أَكْبَرُ مِنْ كَلْبِهَا "my dog is bigger than her dog"

بَقَرَتُهَا أَكْبَرُ مِنْ بَقَرَتِي "her cow is bigger than my cow";

كَلْبَاهُ أَكْبَرُ مِنْ كَلْبَيْهَا "his two dogs are bigger than her two dogs"

(2) The comparative form is also used for the superlative. In this case it is always defined by the article e .g. هُوَ الْأَكْبَرُ "he is the biggest", or by a following genitive e.g.

هُوَ أَكْبَرُ التَّلَامِيذِ "he is the biggest pupil (literally: "the biggest of the pupils"), or by a pronominal suffix e. g.

هُوَ أَكْبَرُهُمْ "he is the biggest of them".

The feminine of the superlative is always on the pattern of كُبْرَى e.g. هِيَ السُّمْنَى "she is the fattest"; هِيَ الصُّغْرَى "she is the smallest".

(3) The adjectives denoting colours or bodily defects have, in the masculine, the same form as comparatives. For example:

وَلَدٌ أَخْرَسُ "a dumb child"; كَلْبٌ أَحْمَرُ "a red dog";

The feminine of these adjectives has the form of حَمْرَاءُ

and the plural of these has the form of حُمْرٌ e. g.

بِنْتٌ خَرْسَاءُ "a dumb girl"; شَجَرَةٌ خَضْرَاءُ "a green tree";

أَوْلَادٌ خُرْسٌ "dumb children".

Note : بَقَرَةٌ حَمْرَاءُ "a red cow" — بَقَرَتَانِ حَمْرَاوَانِ "two red cows" — In the Dual the **Hamza** of the fem. sing. is changed into و

Fifty-third Lesson

١. بَقَرَتِي أَكْبَرُ مِنْ بَقَرَتِكَ. هِيَ ٱلْكُبْرَى فِي هٰذِهِ ٱلْقَرْيَةِ ٢. لِي بَقَرَتَانِ حَمْرَاوَانِ وَلَكَ بَقَرَتَانِ سَوْدَاوَانِ ٣. ذَبَحَ جَارِي ٱلْيَوْمَ خَرُوفَيْنِ وَوَزَّعَ ٱللَّحْمَ مَجَّانًا بَيْنَ فُقَرَاءِ هٰذِهِ ٱلْحَارَةِ ٤. فَتَحَ جَارُنَا دُكَّانَ سَمَكٍ فِي ٱلسُّوقِ ٱلَّذِي فِي ٱلْمَدِينَةِ ٱلْقَدِيمَةِ ٥. هٰؤُلَاءِ ٱلْأَوْلَادُ خُرْسٌ وَأُولَائِكَ ٱلْأَوْلَادُ طُرْشٌ ٦. جَارُنَا ثَوْرٌ كَبِيرٌ وَسَمِينٌ. هُوَ ٱلْأَكْبَرُ وَٱلْأَسْمَنُ فِي قَرْيَتِنَا ٧. أَخِي إِبْرٰهِيمُ يَدْرُسُ فِي ٱلْمَدْرَسَةِ ٱلْجَدِيدَةِ. هُوَ أَصْغَرُ ٱلتَّلَامِيذِ فِيهَا ٨. لِأَخِي ٱلْكَبِيرِ سَيَّارَتَانِ كَبِيرَتَانِ ٱشْتَرَاهُمَا فِي ٱلْقُدْسِ فِي ٱلسَّنَةِ ٱلْمَاضِيَةِ ٩. ٱلدُّرُوسُ فِي هٰذَا ٱلْكِتَابِ سَهْلَةٌ وَٱلدُّرُوسُ فِي ذٰلِكَ ٱلْكِتَابِ صَعْبَةٌ ١٠. هٰذِهِ ٱلدُّرُوسُ أَسْهَلُ مِنْ تِلْكَ ٱلدُّرُوسِ ١١. هٰذَا ٱلْكُرْسِيُّ ثَقِيلٌ وَذٰلِكَ ٱلْكُرْسِيُّ خَفِيفٌ ١٢. هٰذَا ٱلْكُرْسِيُّ أَثْقَلُ مِنْ

١٣. ذٰلِكَ ٱلْكُرْسِيّ. ذٰلِكَ ٱلْكُرْسِيّ أَخَفُّ مِنْ هٰذَا

ٱلْكُرْسِيّ. ١٤. لِي بَيْتٌ جَدِيدٌ وَلِأَخِي بَيْتٌ جَدِيدٌ.

بَيْتُ أَخِي أَجَدُّ مِنْ بَيْتِي. ١٥. أُخْتَا جَارِنَا ٱلْخُرْسَاوَانِ

زَارَتَا ٱلْيَوْمَ أُخْتِي ٱلْكَبِيرَةَ.

Vocabulary: 455. وَزَّعَ •to distribute• (Imperfect: يُوَزِّعُ)

456. مَجَّانًا •gratis• 457. سَمَكٌ •fish•. 458. أَخْرَسُ •dumb•

459. أَطْرَشُ •deaf• 460. دَرْسٌ •lesson• (plural: دُرُوسٌ)

461. سَهْلٌ •easy• 462. صَعْبٌ •difficult• 463. أَخَفُّ is the

comparative of خَفِيفٌ •light (in weight)• 464. أَجَدُّ is the

comparative of جَدِيدٌ •new•.

Translate: 1. His two camels are bigger than our two
camels. 2. Our horse is the biggest horse in this village. 3. My
brother bought yesterday two white cows 4. These two white
cows are fat 5. This pupil is lazy and that pupil is diligent
6. I have red ink and she has blue ink 7. Where did thy
(masc.) friend buy the red ink ? — He bought the red ink in the
new shop 8. The lessons to-day are difficult 9. These lessons
are easier than those lessons 10. Who opened this big
window ?— The pupil of my brother opened it 11. Where is
the white cow which I bought yesterday ? — The white cow is
in the garden of thy (masc.) grand-father 12. This table is
heavy and that table is light 13. That table is lighter than
this table 14. This table is heavier than this table.

Fifty-fourth Lesson

اَلدُّكَّانُ اَلْجَدِيدُ

فَتَحَ رَجُلٌ دُكَّانَ سَمَكٍ . وَعَلَّقَ فَوْقَ بَابِهِ
لَوْحًا صَغِيرًا كَتَبَ عَلَيْهِ : «هُنَا يُبَاعُ اَلسَّمَكُ» .
جَاءَ أَحَدُ أَصْدِقَائِهِ وَقَالَ لَهُ: لِمَاذَا كَتَبْتَ عَلَى
اَللَّوْحِ اَلْكَلِمَةَ «هُنَا» أَلَا يُبَاعُ اَلسَّمَكُ إِلَّا فِي
دُكَّانِكَ؟ فَحَذَفَ صَاحِبُ اَلدُّكَّانِ اَلْكَلِمَةَ «هُنَا» .
ثُمَّ جَاءَ صَدِيقٌ آخَرُ فَقَالَ لِصَاحِبِ اَلدُّكَّانِ: لِمَاذَا
كَتَبْتَ عَلَى اَللَّوْحِ اَلْكَلِمَةَ «يُبَاعُ» أَلَا يَفْهَمُ
اَلنَّاسُ أَنَّكَ لَا تُوَزِّعُ اَلسَّمَكَ مَجَّانًا. فَحَذَفَ
اَلْكَلِمَةَ «يُبَاعُ». ثُمَّ جَاءَ صَدِيقٌ ثَالِثٌ وَقَالَ: لِمَاذَا
كَتَبْتَ اَلْكَلِمَةَ «سَمَك» أَلَا يَرَاهُ اَلنَّاسُ وَلَا
يَشُمُّونَهُ. فَنَزَعَ صَاحِبُ اَلدُّكَّانِ اَللَّوْحَ.

Vocabulary: 465. عَلَّقَ "to hang" 466. لَوْحٌ "board", "plate"
467. يُبَاعُ "is sold" 468. كَلِمَة "word" 469. حَذَفَ "to subtract"
470. ثَالِثٌ "third" 471. شَمَّ "to smell" 472. نَزَعَ (يَنْزِعُ)
"to remove", "to take away".

Fifty-fifth Lesson

The Cardinal Numbers

A. The numerals too have each a masculine form and a feminine form as follows:

Arabic ciphers	Translation	Feminine numerals	Masculine numerals
١	one	وَاحِدَةٌ (إِحْدَى)	وَاحِدٌ (أَحَدٌ)
٢	two	إِثْنَتَانِ	إِثْنَانِ
٣	three	ثَلَاثٌ	ثَلَاثَةٌ (ثَلْثَةٌ)
٤	four	أَرْبَعٌ	أَرْبَعَةٌ
٥	five	خَمْسٌ	خَمْسَةٌ
٦	six	سِتٌّ	سِتَّةٌ
٧	seven	سَبْعٌ	سَبْعَةٌ
٨	eight	ثَمَانٍ	ثَمَانِيَةٌ
٩	nine	تِسْعٌ	تِسْعَةٌ
١٠	ten	عَشْرٌ	عَشَرَةٌ
١١	eleven	إِحْدَى عَشْرَةَ	أَحَدَ عَشَرَ
١٢	twelve	إِثْنَتَا عَشْرَةَ	إِثْنَا عَشَرَ

Arabic ciphers	Translation	Feminine numerals	Masculine numerals
١٣	thirteen	ثَلَاثَ عَشْرَةَ	ثَلَاثَةَ عَشَرَ
١٤	fourteen	أَرْبَعَ عَشْرَةَ	أَرْبَعَةَ عَشَرَ
١٥	fifteen	خَمْسَ عَشْرَةَ	خَمْسَةَ عَشَرَ
١٦	sixteen	سِتَّ عَشْرَةَ	سِتَّةَ عَشَرَ
١٧	seventeen	سَبْعَ عَشْرَةَ	سَبْعَةَ عَشَرَ
١٨	eighteen	ثَمَانِيَ عَشْرَةَ	ثَمَانِيَةَ عَشَرَ
١٩	nineteen	تِسْعَ عَشْرَةَ	تِسْعَةَ عَشَرَ
٢٠	twenty	عِشْرُونَ	
٣٠	thirty	ثَلَاثُونَ	
٤٠	fourty	أَرْبَعُونَ	
٥٠	fifty	خَمْسُونَ	
٦٠	sixty	سِتُّونَ	
٧٠	seventy	سَبْعُونَ	
٨٠	eighty	ثَمَانُونَ	
٩٠	ninety	تِسْعُونَ	
١٠٠	hundred	مِائَةٌ (مِئَةٌ)	

masculine and feminine

مِائَتَانِ (مِثَتَانِ or) 200 (٢٠٠)؛ ثَلَاثُمِائَةٍ (ثَلْثُمِئَةٍ or

300 (٣٠٠)؛ أَرْبَعُمِائَةٍ 400 (٤٠٠)؛ خَمْسُمِائَةٍ 500 (٥٠٠)؛

سِتُّمِائَةٍ 600 (٦٠٠)؛ سَبْعُمِائَةٍ 700 (٧٠٠)؛ ثَمَانِيمِائَةٍ 800

(٨٠٠)؛ تِسْعُمِائَةٍ 900 (٩٠٠)

أَلْفٌ 1000 (١٠٠٠)؛ أَلْفَانِ 2000 (٢٠٠٠)؛ ثَلَاثَةُ آلَافٍ

3000 (٣٠٠٠)؛ أَرْبَعَةُ آلَافٍ 4000 (٤٠٠٠)؛ خَمْسَةُ آلَافٍ

5000 (٥٠٠٠)

أَحَدَ عَشَرَ أَلْفًا 11000 (١١،٠٠٠)؛ إِثْنَا عَشَرَ أَلْفًا

12000 (١٢،٠٠٠)؛ ثَلَاثَةَ عَشَرَ أَلْفًا 13000 (١٣،٠٠٠)؛

عِشْرُونَ أَلْفًا 20000 (٢٠،٠٠٠)؛ خَمْسُونَ أَلْفًا 50000

(٥٠،٠٠٠)؛ مِئَةُ أَلْفٍ 100 000 (١٠٠،٠٠٠)؛ أَلْفُ أَلْفٍ

(مَلْيُونٌ or) 1.000.000 (١،٠٠٠،٠٠٠)؛ صِفْرٌ Zero.

B. In compound numbers from 21 to 99 the units are put
before the tens and are connected by وَ ("and"), the units having
each a masculine or a feminine form e. g.

ثَلَاثَةٌ وَسِتُّونَ 63 (masc.)، ثَلَاثٌ وَسِتُّونَ 63 (fem.)؛

خَمْسَةٌ وَسَبْعُونَ 75 (masc.)، خَمْسٌ وَسَبْعُونَ 75 (fem.)؛

سِتَّةٌ وَتِسْعُونَ 96 (masc.)، سِتٌّ وَتِسْعُونَ 96 (fem.)؛

In compound numbers of thousands, hundreds, tens and units the largest number is put first, but the units are put before the tens e g.

(١،٢٢٣) 1223 أَلْفٌ وَمِائَتَانِ وَثَلَاثَةٌ وَعِشْرُونَ

(٢،٥٣٤) 2534 أَلْفَانِ وَخَمْسُمِائَةٍ وَأَرْبَعَةٌ وَثَلَاثُونَ

(١٥،٤٧٦) 15476 خَمْسَةَ عَشَرَ أَلْفًا وَأَرْبَعُمِئَةٍ وَسِتٌّ وَسَبْعُونَ

C. (1) The numeral 1 follows the noun e. g.

"one cow" (fem.) بَقَرَةٌ وَاحِدَةٌ "one ass" (masc.); حِمَارٌ وَاحِدٌ

The numeral أَحَدُ "one„ (fem. إِحْدَى) is used only before a plural in genitive and is to be translated "one of the..." e. g.

"one of the men" , إِحْدَى النِّسَاءِ "one of أَحَدُ الرِّجَالِ the women".

(2) إِثْنَانِ (fem. إِثْنَتَانِ) "is used only without a noun e. g.

"how كَمْ حِمَارًا لَهُ وَكَمْ لَهَا؟ — لَهُ إِثْنَانِ وَلَهَا ثَلَاثَةٌ many asses has he and how many has she ? — he has two and she has three".

إِثْنَانِ "two" (fem. إِثْنَتَانِ) is not used with a noun because the Dual of the noun itself denotes the number "two" e. g. حِمَارَانِ "two asses"; بَقَرَتَانِ "two cows".

(3) The numerals 3—10 are followed by the noun in the Genitive Plural e. g. ثَلَاثَةُ كُتُبٍ "three books„; أَرْبَعَةُ كِلَابٍ "four dogs"; خَمْسَةُ مُعَلِّمِينَ "five teachers" etc.

(4) The numerals 11—19 are followed by the noun in the Accus.

Sing. e. g. "11 asses"; أَحَدَ عَشَرَ حِمَارًا ثَـلَاثَـةً

"43 books"; ثَلَاثٌ وَأَرْبَعُونَ بَقَرَةً وَأَرْبَعُونَ كِتَابًا

"43 cows".

(5) The numerals 100, 1000 are followed by the noun in the

Gen. Sing. e. g. "100 years"; مِئَةُ سَنَةٍ خَمْسُمِائَةِ سَنَةٍ

"500 years"; "1000 books"; أَلْفُ كِتَابٍ أَلْفَا كِتَابٍ

"2000 books"

Note : "120 books"; مِائَةٌ وَعِشْرُونَ كِتَابًا مِائَةٌ

وَخَمْسَةُ كُتُبٍ "105 books".

D. The numerals 11—19 are indeclinable e. g.

"11 books"; أَحَدَ عَشَرَ كِتَابًا فِي أَحَدَ عَشَرَ كِتَابًا

"in 11 books"; قَرَأْتُ أَحَدَ عَشَرَ كِتَابًا "I read 11 books".

Exception : (fem. إِثْنَتَا عَشْرَةَ) إِثْنَا عَشَرَ which is

in the Gen. and in the Acc. إِثْنَيْ عَشَرَ

(fem. إِثْنَتَيْ عَشْرَةَ).

The other numerals are declinable e. g. فِي خَمْسَةِ كُتُبٍ

"I read 5 books"; قَرَأْتُ خَمْسَةَ كُتُبٍ "in five books";

قَرَأْتُ عِشْرِينَ كِتَابًا "in 20 books; فِي عِشْرِينَ كِتَابًا

قَرَأْتُ خَمْسَةً وَعِشْرِينَ كِتَابًا. "I read 20 books."

قَرَأْتُ مِائَتَيْنِ وَخَمْسَةَ كُتُبٍ. "I read 205 books"

Fifty-sixth Lesson

١. لِأَخِي ٱلْكَبِيرِ سَيَّارَتَانِ كَبِيرَتَانِ إِحْدَاهُمَا سَيَّارَةُ رُكَّابٍ وَٱلْأُخْرَى سَيَّارَةُ شَحْنٍ. ٢. فِي ٱلْأُسْبُوعِ سَبْعَةُ أَيَّامٍ وَهِيَ: يَوْمُ ٱلْأَحَدِ وَيَوْمُ ٱلِٱثْنَيْنِ وَيَوْمُ ٱلثَّلَاثَاءِ وَيَوْمُ ٱلْأَرْبَعَاءِ وَيَوْمُ ٱلْخَمِيسِ وَيَوْمُ ٱلْجُمْعَةِ وَيَوْمُ ٱلسَّبْتِ. ٣. فِي ٱلْيَوْمِ أَرْبَعٌ وَعِشْرُونَ سَاعَةً وَفِي ٱلسَّاعَةِ سِتُّونَ دَقِيقَةً وَفِي نِصْفِ ٱلسَّاعَةِ ثَلَاثُونَ دَقِيقَةً وَفِي رُبْعِ ٱلسَّاعَةِ خَمْسَ عَشْرَةَ دَقِيقَةً وَفِي ثُلْثِ ٱلسَّاعَةِ عِشْرُونَ دَقِيقَةً. أَمَّا ٱلدَّقِيقَةُ فَفِيهَا سِتُّونَ ثَانِيَةً. ٤. فِي كُلِّ جُنَيْهٍ فَلَسْطِينِيٍّ مِائَةُ غِرْشٍ وَفِي كُلِّ غِرْشٍ عَشَرَةُ مِلَّاتٍ. ٥. بِكَمِ ٱشْتَرَيْتَ ٱلْيَوْمَ تُفَّاحًا وَبِكَمِ ٱشْتَرَيْتَ عِنَبًا؟ - إِشْتَرَيْتُ ٱلْيَوْمَ تُفَّاحًا بِسَبْعَةِ غُرُوشٍ وَعِنَبًا بِثَلَاثَةَ عَشَرَ غِرْشًا. ٦. بِكَمِ ٱشْتَرَيْتَ هٰذَيْنِ ٱلدَّفْتَرَيْنِ؟ - إِشْتَرَيْتُ أَحَدُهُمَا بِسِتَّةِ

مِلَاتٍ وَٱلْآخَرَ ٱشْتَرَيْتُ بِعِشْرِينَ مِلًّا .٧ إِبْنُ كَمْ
أَنْتَ (أَوْ : عُمْرُكَ كَمْ سَنَةً) ؟– أَنَا ٱبْنُ خَمْسَ
عَشْرَةَ سَنَةً (أَوْ : عُمْرِي خَمْسَ عَشْرَةَ سَنَةً) .٨ أَنَا ٱبْنُ
خَمْسٍ وَعِشْرِينَ سَنَةً (أَوْ : عُمْرِي خَمْسٌ وَعِشْرُونَ
سَنَةً) وَأَخِي ٱلْكَبِيرُ ٱبْنُ ثَلَاثٍ وَثَلَاثِينَ سَنَةً
(أَوْ : وَعُمْرُ أَخِي ٱلْكَبِيرِ ثَلَاثٌ وَثَلَاثُونَ سَنَةً)
.٩ إِشْتَرَيْتُ ٱلْيَوْمَ أَرْبَعَةَ كُتُبٍ جَدِيدَةٍ وَأَخِي
ٱشْتَرَى ٱثْنَيْ عَشَرَ كِتَابًا .١٠ أَخِي ٱلصَّغِيرُ كَانَ فِي
يَافَا مَرَّتَيْنِ وَفِي حَيْفَا أَرْبَعَ مَرَّاتٍ وَفِي ٱلْقُدْسِ
ٱثْنَتَيْ عَشْرَةَ مَرَّةً.

Vocabulary: 473. رَاكِبٌ "passenger" (plural : رُكَّابٌ)

474. شَحْنٌ "freight", "cargo", "load" 475. أُسْبُوعٌ (or : جُمْعَةٌ)
"week" (plural : أَسَابِيعُ) 476. يَوْمُ ٱلْأَحَدِ "Sunday"

477. يَوْمُ ٱلِٱثْنَيْنِ "Monday" 478. يَوْمُ ٱلثَّلَاثَاءِ "Tuesday"

479. يَوْمُ ٱلْأَرْبَعَاءِ "Wednesday" 480. يَوْمُ ٱلْخَمِيسِ "Thursday"

481. يَوْمُ ٱلْجُمْعَةِ "Friday" 482. يَوْمُ ٱلسَّبْتِ "Saturday"

483. دَقِيقَةٌ "minute" (plural : دَقَائِقُ) 484. نِصْفٌ (and نُصْفٌ)

ثَانِيَةٌ 487 ⅓ ثُلُثٌ 486. "quarter" رُبْعٌ 485. "half"

غِرْشٌ "piastre" 489. "pound" جُنَيْهٌ 488. (ثَوَانٍ : plural)

أَوْ 491. (مِلَّاتٌ : plural) مِلٌّ "mil" 490. (غُرُوشٌ : plural)

"or" 492. (عُمْرُهُ كَمْ سَنَةً or) إِبْنُ كَمْ هُوَ "how old

is he?" 493. (عُمْرُهُ سَنَتَانِ or) هُوَ ابْنُ سَنَتَيْنِ "he is two

years old".

١. فِي هٰذَا ٱلشَّارِعِ خَمْسَةٌ وَأَرْبَعُونَ بَيْتًا وَفِي
ذٰلِكَ ٱلشَّارِعِ سَبْعَةٌ وَعِشْرُونَ بَيْتًا ٢. أَيْنَ تَعَلَّمْتَ
ٱللُّغَةَ ٱلْعَرَبِيَّةَ ؟ــ تَعَلَّمْتُهَا فِي مَدْرَسَةٍ مَسَائِيَّةٍ ٣. فِي
هٰذِهِ ٱلْمَدِينَةِ أَرْبَعُ مَدَارِسَ مَسَائِيَّةٍ لِتَعْلِيمِ ٱلْعُمَّالِ
ٱلْقِرَاءَةَ وَٱلْكِتَابَةَ ٤. هَلْ يَعْرِفُ هٰذَا ٱلْفَلَّاحُ ٱلْقِرَاءَةَ
وَٱلْكِتَابَةَ ؟ــ لَا هٰذَا ٱلْفَلَّاحُ لَا يَعْرِفُ لَا ٱلْقِرَاءَةَ
وَلَا ٱلْكِتَابَةَ هُوَ أُمِّيٌّ ٥. إِقْرَأْ يَا أَحْمَدُ مَا كَتَبْتُ
عَلَى ٱللَّوْحِ ٦. قَالَ ٱلْمُعَلِّمُ لِتِلْمِيذِهِ اقْرَأْ يَا إِبْرٰهِيمُ مَا
كَتَبَ زَيْدٌ عَلَى ٱللَّوْحِ ٧. فِي هٰذِهِ ٱلْمَدْرَسَةِ ٱلْمَسَائِيَّةِ
سِتَّةٌ وَخَمْسُونَ تِلْمِيذًا ٨. زَوْجَةُ جَارِنَا لَا تَعْرِفُ
ٱلْقِرَاءَةَ وَلَا ٱلْكِتَابَةَ هِيَ أُمِّيَّةٌ ٩. زَوْجُ هٰذِهِ

ٱلِامْرَأَةِ يَدْرُسُ ٱللُّغَةَ ٱلْعَرَبِيَّةَ فِي إِحْدَى ٱلْمَدَارِسِ
ٱلْمَسَائِيَّةِ. 10. لِأَبِي ٱثْنَتَا عَشْرَةَ بَقَرَةً وَخَمْسَةُ جِمَالٍ.

Vocabulary: 494. مَدْرَسَةٌ مَسَائِيَّةٌ "evening school"

495. تَعْلِيم "instruction" 496. عَامِلٌ "workman", "doer" (plur. عُمَّالٌ)

497. قِرَاءَةٌ "reading" 498. كِتَابَةٌ "writing" 499. أُمِّيٌّ "illiterate"

(fem. أُمِّيَّةٌ) 500. The Alif in إِقْرَأْ is **Hamzat-l-wasl** 501. زَوْجٌ

"husband" 502. زَوْجَةٌ "wife" 503. إِمْرَأَةٌ "woman".

Translate: 1. How many pupils are there in this school ?
— In this school there are ninety-four pupils   2. My grand-
mother has three big dogs and my uncle (on the mother's side) has
two dogs   3. In this book there are sixty lessons and in
that book there are sixty-seven lessons   4. In this room there
are four windows and in the room of my sister there are three
windows 5. In the after-noon I bought five books in the new
shop   6. How many books has thy (masc.) pupil ? — He has
fourteen books   7. How old is the brother of our neighbour?
— he is nineteen years old   8. This peasant is illiterate and
his wife too is illiterate. 9. How many times was our neighbour
in Jaffa ? — He was there twice or three times   10. I read this
book twice and my sister read it once   11. In this village
there are two evening schools.

Fifty-seventh Lesson

أَلشَّيْخُ وَٱلْمَلِكُ

رَأَى مَلِكٌ شَيْخًا وَاحِدًا يَغْرِسُ نَخْلًا. فَقَالَ لَهُ:
أَيُّهَا ٱلشَّيْخُ أَتُؤَمِّلُ أَنْ تَأْكُلَ مِنْ ثَمَرِ هٰذَا ٱلنَّخْلِ

وَهُوَ لَا يُثْمِرُ إِلَّا بَعْدَ سِنِينَ كَثِيرَةٍ.

فَقَالَ الشَّيْخُ: أَغْرِسُ النَّخْلَ لِيَأْكُلَ أَحْفَادِي مِنْ ثَمَرِهِ كَمَا أَكَلْتُ أَنَا مِمَّا غَرَسَ جَدِّي.

فَاسْتَحْسَنَ الْمَلِكُ ذَلِكَ وَأَعْطَاهُ عِشْرِينَ دِينَارًا.

فَأَخَذَهَا الشَّيْخُ وَقَالَ: أَيُّهَا الْمَلِكُ لَقَدْ أَكَلْتُ أَنَا بِنَفْسِي مِنْ ثَمَرِ هَذَا النَّخْلِ. فَتَعَجَّبَ الْمَلِكُ مِنْ كَلَامِهِ وَأَعْطَاهُ عِشْرِينَ دِينَارًا أُخْرَى.

فَأَخَذَهَا وَقَالَ: أَيُّهَا الْمَلِكُ وَأَعْجَبُ مِنْ كُلِّ شَيْءٍ أَنَّ النَّخْلَ قَدْ أَثْمَرَ السَّنَةَ مَرَّتَيْنِ. فَتَعَجَّبَ الْمَلِكُ مِنْ كَلَامِهِ وَأَعْطَاهُ عِشْرِينَ دِينَارًا أُخْرَى.

Vocabulary: 504. أَيُّهَا is a vocative particle 505. أَمَّلَ
"to hope" (Imperf. يُؤَمِّلُ) 506. ثَمَرٌ "fruit" 507. أَثْمَرَ "to bear
fruit", "to produce fruit" (Imperfect يُثْمِرُ) 508. كَمَا "as", "just as"
509. دِينَارٌ "Dinar" 510. اِسْتَحْسَنَ "to approve" "to appreciate"
511. نَفْسٌ "soul", "self" (أَنَا بِنَفْسِي "myself") 512. تَعَجَّبَ مِنْ
"to wonder at" 513. عَجِيبٌ "wonderful".

Fifty-eighth Lesson

The Ordinal Numbers

Translation	Feminine	Masculine
the first	اَلْأُولَى	اَلْأَوَّلُ
the second	اَلثَّانِيَةُ	اَلثَّانِي
the third	اَلثَّالِثَةُ	اَلثَّالِثُ
the fourth	اَلرَّابِعَةُ	اَلرَّابِعُ
the fifth	اَلْخَامِسَةُ	اَلْخَامِسُ
the sixth	اَلسَّادِسَةُ	اَلسَّادِسُ
the seventh	اَلسَّابِعَةُ	اَلسَّابِعُ
the eighth	اَلثَّامِنَةُ	اَلثَّامِنُ
the ninth	اَلتَّاسِعَةُ	اَلتَّاسِعُ
the tenth	اَلْعَاشِرَةُ	اَلْعَاشِرُ
the eleventh	اَلْحَادِيَةَ عَشْرَةَ	اَلْحَادِيَ عَشَرَ
the twelfth	اَلثَّانِيَةَ عَشْرَةَ	اَلثَّانِي عَشَرَ
the thirteenth	اَلثَّالِثَةَ عَشْرَةَ	اَلثَّالِثَ عَشَرَ
the fourteenth	اَلرَّابِعَةَ عَشْرَةَ	اَلرَّابِعَ عَشَرَ
etc.	etc.	etc.

For the ordinals from 20 on the cardinal numbers are used e. g.

أَلْبَيْتُ ٱلْعِشْرُونَ "the twentieth house",

أَلْبَيْتُ ٱلْمِائَةُ وَٱلْأَرْبَعُونَ "the hundred and fortieth house"

The compound ordinals of the tens and units are as follows:

	Masculine	Feminine
the 21st	أَلْحَادِى وَٱلْعِشْرُونَ	أَلْحَادِيَةُ وَٱلْعِشْرُونَ
the 32nd	أَلثَّانِي وَٱلثَّلَاثُونَ	أَلثَّانِيَةُ وَٱلثَّلَاثُونَ
the 54th	أَلرَّابِعُ وَٱلْخَمْسُونَ	أَلرَّابِعَةُ وَٱلْخَمْسُونَ
etc.	etc.	etc.

The ordinals from 11—19 are indeclinable e. g.

فِي ٱلْبَيْتِ ٱلْحَادِيَ عَشَرَ "in the 11th house";

فِي ٱلْمَدْرَسَةِ ٱلثَّالِثَةَ عَشْرَةَ "in the 13th school".

١. أَلدَّرْسُ ٱلْعَاشِرُ فِي هٰذَا ٱلْكِتَابِ أَسْهَلُ مِنَ ٱلدَّرْسِ ٱلسَّادِسَ عَشَرَ وَٱلدَّرْسُ ٱلثَّالِثُ وَٱلْخَمْسُونَ أَصْعَبُ مِنَ ٱلدَّرْسِ ٱلْحَادِيَ عَشَرَ ٢. حَرَثَ هٰذَا ٱلْفَلَّاحُ حَقْلَهُ ٱلْيَوْمَ مِنَ ٱلسَّاعَةِ ٱلْخَامِسَةِ صَبَاحًا إِلَى ٱلسَّاعَةِ ٱلْحَادِيَةَ عَشْرَةَ ٣. أَخِي يَحْرُثُ حَقْلَهُ مَرَّتَيْنِ فِي كُلِّ يَوْمٍ ٱلْمَرَّةَ ٱلْأُولَى مِنَ ٱلسَّاعَةِ

ٱلسَّادِسَةِ صَبَاحًا وَٱلْمَرَّةَ ٱلثَّانِيَةَ مِنَ ٱلسَّاعَةِ ٱلثَّالِثَةِ

إِلَى ٱلسَّاعَةِ ٱلْخَامِسَةِ بَعْدَ ٱلظُّهْرِ ٤. قَدْ أُنْشِئَتْ فِي

هٰذِهِ ٱلْمَدِينَةِ جَمْعِيَّةٌ لِمُحَارَبَةِ ٱلْأُمِّيَّةِ ٥. غَايَةُ هٰذِهِ

ٱلْجَمْعِيَّةِ هِيَ مُحَارَبَةُ ٱلْأُمِّيَّةِ ٦. إِشْتَرَى ٱلْفَلَّاحُ فِي

هٰذَا ٱلدُّكَّانِ مِنْجَلًا وَزَوْجَتُهُ ٱشْتَرَتْ فِيهِ سِكِّينًا

٧. ذٰلِكَ ٱلْكِتَابُ مُؤَلَّفٌ مِنْ ثَلَاثَةِ أَجْزَاءٍ. فِي

ٱلْجُزْءِ ٱلْأَوَّلِ مِائَتَانِ وَخَمْسٌ وَعِشْرُونَ صَفْحَةً وَفِي

ٱلْجُزْءِ ٱلثَّانِي ثَلَاثُمِائَةٍ وَأَرْبَعٌ وَسِتُّونَ صَفْحَةً وَفِي

ٱلْجُزْءِ ٱلثَّالِثِ مِائَتَانِ وَسِتٌّ وَثَمَانُونَ صَفْحَةً.

Vocabulary: 514. حَرَثَ "to plough" (Imperf. (يَحْرُثُ)

515. أُنْشِئَ "to be created" 516. جَمْعِيَّةٌ "society" 517. مُحَارَبَةٌ

"combat", "oppose" 518. غَايَةٌ "object"; 519. أُمِّيَّةٌ "illiterateness"

520. سِكِّينٌ "end" 521. مِنْجَلٌ (مَنَاجِلُ plur.) "sickle", "scythe"

"knife" (plur. سَكَاكِينُ) 522. مُؤَلَّفٌ مِنْ "is composed of"

523. جُزْءٌ "part" (plur. أَجْزَاءٌ) 524. صَفْحَةٌ "page".,

<u>Translate:</u> 1. The book of my brother is composed of two parts, in the first part there are three hundred and fifty-five pages and in the second part there are four hundred and thirty nine pages 2. I was yester-day in Jerusalem from eight o'clock in the morning until three o'clock after-noon 3. The sixteenth lesson in this book is more difficult than the thirty-seventh lesson 4. Where is the second part of this English book? — It is in my room on the table 5. When has thy (masc.) brother written his Arabic lessons? — he wrote them from six to eight o'clock in the evening 6. How many camels has your (masc.) grand-father? — Our grand-father has twenty-five camels 7. Where is the third part of this book? — It is in the room of our sister 8. What has thy (masc.) sister written in the after-noon? — She has written the sixteenth lesson 9. This lesson is easier than the twenty-eighth lesson 10. How many lessons are there in this book? — In this book there are fifty-seven lessons.

Fifty-ninth Lesson

مُحَارَبَةُ الْأُمِّيَّة

أُنْشِئَتْ جَمْعِيَّةٌ فِي أَحَدِ الْمُدُنِ غَايَتُهَا مُحَارَبَةُ الْأُمِّيَّةِ.

فَفَتَحَتْ هٰذِهِ الْجَمْعِيَّةُ مَدَارِسَ لَيْلِيَّةً فِي الْقُرَى

وَالْمُدُنِ لِتَعْلِيمِ الْفَلَّاحِينَ وَالْعُمَّالِ الْقِرَاءَةَ وَالْكِتَابَةَ.

فَأَرْسَلَتْ هٰذِهِ الْجَمْعِيَّةُ يَوْمًا مُفَتِّشًا إِلَى إِحْدَى

الْقُرَى يَحْمِلُ الْهَدَايَا لِلَّذِينَ يَتَعَلَّمُونَ فِي هٰذِهِ

الْمَدَارِسِ اللَّيْلِيَّةِ تَشْجِيعًا لَهُمْ. فَاجْتَمَعَ الْفَلَّاحُونَ

حَوْلَهُ. فَدَعَا الْمُفَتِّشُ امْرَأَةً مِنْهُمْ وَطَلَبَ مِنْهَا أَنْ

تَقْرَأَ كَلِمَةً أَشَارَ إِلَيْهَا فِي كِتَابٍ كَانَ فِي يَدِهِ.

فَقَرَأَتْ بِصَوْتٍ عَالٍ «مِنْدِيل» فَقَالَ لَهَا: أَحْسَنْتِ
وَأَعْطَاهَا مِنْدِيلاً. ثُمَّ دَعَا رَجُلاً: فَقَرَأَ بِسُرْعَةٍ «مِنْجَل».
فَقَالَ الْمُفَتِّشْ: أَحْسَنْتَ وَأَعْطَاهُ مِنْجَلاً.

ثُمَّ دَعَا آخَرَ وَطَلَبَ مِنْهُ أَنْ يَقْرَأَ كَلِمَةً أَشَارَ
إِلَيْهَا. فَقَرَأَ بِسُرْعَةٍ «ثَوْرْ» وَكَانَتِ الْكَلِمَةُ شَيْئاً
آخَرَ. فَقَالَ لَهُ الْمُفَتِّشْ: أَنْظُرْ جَيِّداً وَأَقْرَأَ. فَنَظَرَ
الرَّجُلُ مَرَّةً أُخْرَى وَقَالَ «ثَوْرْ». فَقَامَتْ زَوْجَتُهُ
وَقَالَتْ: زَوْجِي يُحْسِنُ الْقِرَاءَةَ وَلـٰـكِنَّهُ فِي حَاجَةٍ
شَدِيدَةٍ إِلَى ثَوْرٍ يَحْرُثُ بِهِ الْأَرْضَ.

Vocabulary:

525. أَرْسَلَ "to send" (Imperf. يُرْسِلُ)

526. مُفَتِّشْ "inspector" 527. هَدِيَّةٌ "present" (plural: هَدَايَا)

528. تَشْجِيع "encouragement" 529. إِجْتَمَعَ "to be gathered";

530. حَوْلَ "about"; "round" 531. دَعَا "to call", "to assemble"

532. أَحْسَنَ "to do (something) "to invite" (دَعَوْتُ "I called")

533. سُرْعَةٌ "speed", "haste", well" (Imperfect: يُحْسِنُ)

534. نَظَرَ "to look" (Imperative: أَنْظُرْ) "rapidity" 535. (جَيِّدٌ)

536. قَامَ "to stand up", "to rise" "well", "good" 537. حَاجَةٌ "need".

Sixtieth Lesson

اَلرَّجُلُ وَالْمَوْتُ

رَجُلٌ مَرَّةً حَمَلَ حُزْمَةَ حَطَبٍ مِنَ الْغَابَةِ الْقَرِيبَةِ إِلَى بَيْتِهِ. فَثَقُلَتْ عَلَيْهِ. فَلَمَّا تَعِبَ مِنْ حَمْلِهَا رَمَى بِهَا عَنْ كَتِفِهِ وَدَعَا عَلَى نَفْسِهِ بِالْمَوْتِ. فَشَخَصَ لَهُ الْمَوْتُ وَقَالَ: هَا أَنَا ذَا! لِمَاذَا دَعَوْتَنِي؟ فَقَالَ لَهُ الرَّجُلُ دَعَوْتُكَ لِتُحَمِّلَنِي هٰذِهِ حُزْمَةَ الْحَطَبِ عَلَى كَتِفِي.

Vocabulary: 538. مَوْتٌ "death" 539. ثَقُلَ "to be heavy"

540 رَمَى "carrying" 542. حَمْلٌ "to become tired" 541. تَعِبَ

"to throw down" 543. كَتِفٌ "shoulder" 544. شَخَصَ

"to appear" 545. هَا أَنَا ذَا "see, I am here!" 546. حَمَّلَ

"to load", "to charge" (Imperfect: يُحَمِّلُ)

ENGLISH - ARABIC

VOCABULARY

Note 1: This vocabulary is only for the exercises in this book which are to be translated from English into Arabic.

Note 2: About the radical letters of the verbs see page 30, Notes 1—2.

Note 3: About the **Imperfect** see lesson 19.

Note 4: As to the **broken plural** see lesson 41

A

a see lesson 23 (3)	
after	بَعْدَ
also	أَيْضًا
always	دَائِمًا
an see lesson 23 (3)	
and	وَ and فَ (see page 70, Note 2)
animal	حَيَوَانٌ
— plural :	حَيَوَانَاتٌ
to answer	أَجَابَ
— imperfect :	يُجِيبُ
apple	تُفَّاحٌ (see page 112, Note)
Arabic	عَرَبِيٌّ

— the Arabic language	اَللُّغَةُ ٱلْعَرَبِيَّةُ
are and art see is	
as for; as to	أَمَّا
to ask	سَأَلَ
— imperfect :	يَسْأَلُ
to ask for	طَلَبَ
— imperfect :	يَطْلُبُ
ass	حِمَارٌ
— plural :	حَمِيرٌ
aunt	عَمَّةٌ (on the father's side)
	خَالَةٌ (on the mother's side)

B

Baker	خَبَّازٌ
— plural :	خَبَّازُونَ
barber	حَلَّاقٌ
— plural :	حَلَّاقُونَ
to be	كَانَ

— imperfect :	يَكُونُ
bear	دُبٌّ
— plural :	أَدْبَابٌ
to bear	حَمَلَ
— imperfect :	يَحْمِلُ

10 beat ضَرَبَ	— bigger أَكْبَرُ
— imperfect: يَضْرِبُ	bird عُصْفُورٌ
beautiful جَمِيلٌ	— plural : عَصَافِيرُ
because لِأَنَّ	black أَسْوَدُ
— because I لِأَنِّي	— fem. سَوْدَاءُ
— because he لِأَنَّهُ etc.	— plur. سُودٌ
before قَبْلَ (temporal)	blacksmith حَدَّادٌ
أَمَامَ (local)	— plur. حَدَّادُونَ
قُدَّامَ (local)	blue أَزْرَقُ
behind خَلْفَ	— fem. زَرْقَاءُ
10 believe ظَنَّ	— plur. زُرْقٌ
— imperfect: يَظُنُّ	book كِتَابٌ
bench بَنْكٌ	— plur. كُتُبٌ
— plural بُنُوكٌ	boy وَلَدٌ
better than خَيْرٌ مِنْ	— plur. أَوْلَادٌ
between بَيْنَ	bread خُبْزٌ
big كَبِيرٌ	10 break كَسَرَ

– imperfect : يَكْسِرُ	butter زُبْدَةٌ
brother أَخٌ	to buy إِشْتَرَى
– plur. إِخْوَةٌ and إِخْوَانٌ	– I bought إِشْتَرَيْتُ

C

cage قَفَصٌ	cheese جُبْنٌ (see page 112, Note)
– plural : أَقْفَاصٌ	child وَلَدٌ
camel جَمَلٌ	– plural : أَوْلَادٌ
– plural : جَمَالٌ	city مَدِينَةٌ
carpenter نَجَّارٌ	– plural : مُدُنٌ
– plural : نَجَّارُونَ	clean نَظِيفٌ
to carry حَمَلَ	– cleaner أَنْظَفُ
– Imperfect : يَحْمِلُ	clock سَاعَةٌ
cat قِطٌّ and هِرٌّ	– three o'clock أَلسَّاعَةُ ٱلثَّالِثَةُ
– she-cat قِطَّةٌ and هِرَّةٌ	– five o'clock أَلسَّاعَةُ ٱلْخَامِسَةُ
chair كُرْسِيٌّ	cock دِيكٌ
– plural : كَرَاسِيٌّ	– plural : دُيُوكٌ
cheap رَخِيصٌ	coffee قَهْوَةٌ
– cheaper أَرْخَصُ	to come جَاءَ

جِئْتُ — I came	دَفَاتِرُ : plural —
شِرْكَةٌ and شَرِكَةٌ company	بَقَرَةٌ cow
مُؤَلَّفٌ composed	فِنْجَانٌ cup
دَفْتَرٌ copy-book	فَنَاجِينُ : plural —

D

بِنْتٌ and إِبْنَةٌ daughter	صَعْبٌ difficult
بَنَاتٌ : plural —	مُجْتَهِدٌ diligent
يَوْمٌ day	مُدِيرٌ director
أَيَّامٌ : plural —	وَسِخٌ dirty
نَهَارٌ day (opposite of night) —	قَسَمَ divide to
أَطْرَشُ deaf	يَقْسِمُ : Imperfect —
طَرْشَاءُ fem. —	كَلْبٌ dog
طُرْشٌ plur. —	كِلَابٌ : plural —
غَالٍ dear (price)	بَابٌ door
أَغْلَى مِنْ dearer than —	أَبْوَابٌ : plural —
نَزَلَ descend to	شَرِبَ drink to
يَنْزِلُ Imperfect —	يَشْرَبُ : Imperfect —
مُخْتَلِفٌ different	رَسَمَ draw (sketch) to
	يَرْسُمُ : imperfect —

— imperative : أُرْسُمُ

dumb أَخْرَسُ

— fem. خَرْسَاءُ

— plural : خُرْسٌ

E

easy سَهْلٌ

— plural : أَفْيَالٌ

— easier أَسْهَلُ

eleven أَحَدَ عَشَرَ

to eat أَكَلَ

— feminine : إِحْدَى عَشْرَةَ

— imperfect : يَأْكُلُ

— the eleventh أَلْحَادِيَ عَشَرَ

eight ثَمَانِيَةٌ

— feminine : أَلْحَادِيَةَ عَشْرَةَ

— feminine : ثَمَانٍ

English إِنْكِلِيزِيٌّ

— the eighth أَلثَّامِنُ

— the English Language أَللُّغَةُ الْإِنْكِلِيزِيَّةُ

— eighteen ثَمَانِيَةَ عَشَرَ

to enter دَخَلَ

— feminine : ثَمَانِيَ عَشْرَةَ

— imperfect : يَدْخُلُ

— the eighteenth أَلثَّامِنَ عَشَرَ

evening مَسَاءٌ

— eighty ثَمَانُونَ

— evening school مَدْرَسَةٌ مَسَائِيَّةٌ

elephant فِيلٌ

eye عَيْنٌ

F

face وَجْهٌ

far بَعِيدٌ

— plural : وُجُوهٌ

— farther أَبْعَدُ

farmer	فَلَّاحٌ
— plural :	فَلَّاحُونَ
fat	سَمِينٌ
— fatter	أَسْمَنُ
father	وَالِدٌ and أَبٌ
field	حَقْلٌ
— plural :	حُقُولٌ
to find	وَجَدَ
fire-wood	حَطَبٌ
the first	اَلْأَوَّلُ
— feminine :	اَلْأُولَى
fish	سَمَكٌ
five	خَمْسَةٌ
— feminine :	خَمْسٌ
— the fifth	اَلْخَامِسُ
— fifteen	خَمْسَةَ عَشَرَ
— feminine :	خَمْسَ عَشْرَةَ
— fifty	خَمْسُونَ

food	طَعَامٌ
foolish	أَحْمَقُ
foot	رِجْلٌ
forest	غَابَةٌ
fortunate	سَعِيدٌ
four	أَرْبَعَةٌ
— feminine :	أَرْبَعٌ
— the fourth	اَلرَّابِعُ
— fourteen	أَرْبَعَةَ عَشَرَ
— feminine :	أَرْبَعَ عَشْرَةَ
— forty	أَرْبَعُونَ
fox	ثَعْلَبٌ
— plural :	ثَعَالِبُ
Friday	يَوْمُ الْجُمْعَةِ
friend	صَدِيقٌ
— plural :	أَصْدِقَاءُ
from	مِنْ

G

good جَيِّدٌ and طَيِّبٌ

— better than خَيْرٌ مِنْ

grand-father جَدٌّ

grand-mother جَدَّةٌ

grand-son حَفِيدٌ

gratis مَجَّانًا

great كَبِيرٌ

— greater أَكْبَرُ

green أَخْضَرُ

— feminine : خَضْرَاءُ

— plural : خُضْرٌ

garden حَدِيقَةٌ and بُسْتَانٌ

— plural : حَدَائِقُ and بَسَاتِينُ

gate بَابٌ

— plural : أَبْوَابٌ

girl إِبْنَةٌ and بِنْتٌ

— plural : بَنَاتٌ

go ذَهَبَ

— Imperfect : يَذْهَبُ

go out خَرَجَ

— Imperfect : يَخْرُجُ

God أَللهُ

H

haste عَجَلَةٌ and سُرْعَةٌ

— in haste بِسُرْعَةٍ and بِعَجَلَةٍ

to have لِ (See page 15)

— have as auxiliary verb see lesson 11 B.

he هُوَ

— he has لَهُ (See also lesson 11. B)

hair شَعْرٌ

half نِصْفٌ and نُصْفٌ

hand يَدٌ

happy مَسْرُورٌ and سَعِيدٌ

hare أَرْنَبٌ

— plural : أَرَانِبُ

head رَأْسٌ	horse حِصَانٌ
— plural : رُؤُوسٌ	— plural : أَحْصِنَةٌ
to hear سَمِعَ	hour سَاعَةٌ
— Imperfect : يَسْمَعُ	house بَيْتٌ
heart قَلْبٌ	— plural : بُيُوتٌ
— plural : قُلُوبٌ	how ? كَيْفَ
heavy ثَقِيلٌ	— how many ? كَمْ See page 12 vocabulary
— heavier أَثْقَلُ	— how much ? كَمْ
hen دَجَاجَةٌ	— how old ? إِبْنُ كَمْ See page vocabule
her هَا (suffix) See lesson 8 and lesson 48, A. B.	hundred مِئَةٌ and مِائَةٌ
here هُنَا	to hunt صَادَ
him هُ (suffix) See lesson 17	— Imperfect : يَصِيدُ
his هُ (suffix) See lesson 8 and lesson 48, A. B.	hunter صَيَّادٌ
holy مُقَدَّسٌ	— plural : صَيَّادُونَ

I

I أَنَا	ill مَرِيضٌ
— I have لِي (See also lesson 11. B.)	illiterate أُمِّيٌّ
idle كَسْلَانُ	— feminine : أُمِّيَّةٌ

...mediately حَالًا and فِي الْحَالِ	is The copula "is" ("are") is omitted in the Arabic translation e.g.
...portant مُهِمّ	هُوَ كَبِيرٌ "he is big";
فِي	الْأَوْلَادُ فِي الْبُسْتَانِ "the
in front of قُدَّام and أَمَام	children are in the garden".
...k حِبْرٌ	it هُوَ
...spection تَفْتِيشٌ	— feminine : هِيَ
...spector مُفَتِّشٌ	— it in the objective case هُ (suffix)
...on حَدِيدٌ	See lesson 17
	— feminine : هَا (suffix)

J

...affa يَافَا	Jerusalem أَلْقُدْسُ
...ar جَرَّةٌ	just as كَمَا

K

...ey مِفْتَاحٌ	— plural : مَطَابِيخُ
...plural ; مَفَاتِيحُ	knife سِكِّينٌ
...ing مَلِكٌ	— plural : سَكَاكِينُ
...plural : مُلُوكٌ	know عَرَفَ
...itchen مَطْبَخٌ	— Imperfect : يَعْرِفُ

L

laboratory مَعْمَلٌ	to leave تَرَكَ
– plural : مَعَامِلٌ	– Imperfect : يَتْرُكُ
labourer عَامِلٌ	lesson دَرْسٌ
– plural : عُمَّالٌ	– plural : دُرُوسٌ
lady سَيِّدَةٌ	life حَيَاةٌ
– plural : سَيِّدَاتٌ	light خَفِيفٌ
lamb خَرُوفٌ	– lighter أَخَفُّ
– plural : خِرْفَانٌ	line خَطٌّ
lamp قِنْدِيلٌ and مِصْبَاحٌ	– plural : خُطُوطٌ
– plural : قَنَادِيلُ and مَصَابِيحُ	lion أَسَدٌ
language لِسَانٌ and لُغَةٌ	– plural : أُسُودٌ
large وَاسِعٌ and كَبِيرٌ	load شَحْنٌ and حِمْلٌ
to laugh ضَحِكَ	long طَوِيلٌ
– Imperfect : يَضْحَكُ	– longer أَطْوَلُ
lazy كَسْلَانُ	loyal أَمِينٌ ؛ مُخْلِصٌ
to learn دَرَسَ and تَعَلَّمَ	loyalty أَمَانَةٌ ؛ إِخْلَاصٌ
– Imperfect : يَدْرُسُ and يَتَعَلَّمُ	lucky سَعِيدٌ

M

mad مَجْنُونٌ	million مَلْيُونٌ
— plural : مَجَانِينُ	— plural : مَلَايِينُ
man رَجُلٌ	minister وَزِيرٌ
— plural : رِجَالٌ	— plural : وُزَرَاءُ
many كَثِيرٌ	minute دَقِيقَةٌ
— more أَكْثَرُ	— plural : دَقَائِقُ
mariner مَلَّاحٌ	monday يَوْمُ ٱلِاثْنَيْنِ
market سُوقٌ	month شَهْرٌ
— plural : أَسْوَاقٌ	— plur. شُهُورٌ ، أَشْهُرٌ
martyr شَهِيدٌ	moon قَمَرٌ
— plural : شُهَدَاءُ	more أَكْثَرُ
me نِي (suffix) See lesson 17	morning صَبَاحٌ
meat لَحْمٌ	Moslem مُسْلِمٌ
merchant تَاجِرٌ	— plural : مُسْلِمُونَ
— plural : تُجَّارٌ	mosque جَامِعٌ and مَسْجِدٌ
midday أَلظُّهْرُ	— plural : جَوَامِعُ and مَسَاجِدُ
milk حَلِيبٌ	mother وَالِدَةٌ and أُمٌّ

to mount طَلَعَ	much كَثِيرٌ
— Imperfect: يَطْلَعُ	my ي (suffix) See lesson 8 and lesson 48. A. B.

N

name إِسْمٌ This Alif is Hamzat-l-wasl

— plural : أَسْمَاءٌ

narrow ضَيِّقٌ

near قَرِيبٌ

— nearer أَقْرَبُ

necessary لَازِمٌ

neighbour جَارٌ

— plural : جِيرَانٌ

new جَدِيدٌ

newspaper جَرِيدَةٌ

— plural : جَرَائِدُ

night لَيْلٌ

nine تِسْعَةٌ

— feminine : تِسْعُ

— the ninth اَلتَّاسِعُ

— nineteen تِسْعَةَ عَشَرَ

— feminine تِسْعَ عَشْرَةَ

— ninety تِسْعُونَ

— the ninetieth اَلتِّسْعُونَ

no لَا

noon اَلظُّهْرُ

— after-noon بَعْدَ الظُّهْرِ

— before-noon قَبْلَ الظُّهْرِ

north شَمَالٌ ؛ شِمَالٌ

not مَا before the perfect form e. g.

مَا كَتَبَ "he did not write"

لَا before the Imperfect form e. g.

لَا يَكْتُبُ "he does (he will) not write"

number عَدَدٌ

O

O ! يَا Particle of adress	— feminine إِحْدَى
of مِنْ See also lesson 25 (1) b.	to open فَتَحَ
officer ضَابِطٌ	— Imperfect يَفْتَحُ
— plural : ضُبَّاطٌ	or أَوْ
old قَدِيمٌ	the orient الشَّرْقُ
— age كَبِيرُ السِّنِّ	orientalist مُسْتَشْرِقٌ
— man شَيْخٌ See also page 136, Vocabulary	the other الآخَرُ
on عَلَى	— feminine الأُخْرَى
once مَرَّةٌ	our نَا (suffix) See lesson 8 and lesson 48 A. B.
— adverbial : مَرَّةً	ove: فَوْقَ ، عَلَى
one وَاحِدٌ	ox ثَوْرٌ
— feminine : وَاحِدَةٌ	— plural : ثِيَارٌ and أَثْوَارٌ
— one of أَحَدٌ See lesson 55 C. (1)	

P

page صَفْحَةٌ	part جُزْءٌ and قِسْمٌ
— plural : صَفَحَاتٌ	— plural : أَجْزَاءٌ and أَقْسَامٌ
palace سَرَايٌ ، قَصْرٌ	partner شَرِيكٌ
the parents الْوَالِدَانِ	— plural : شُرَكَاءُ

partnership شِرْكَةٌ and شَرَكَةٌ	— imperfect : يَحْرُثُ
the past اَلْمَاضِي	poor فَقِيرٌ
peasant see farmer	— plural : فُقَرَاءُ
pest طَاعُونٌ	— poorer أَفْقَرُ
picture صُورَةٌ	possessor صَاحِبٌ
— plural : صُوَرٌ	— plural : أَصْحَابٌ
piece قِطْعَةٌ	post بَرِيدٌ
— plural : قِطَعٌ	— post office مَكْتَبُ ٱلْبَرِيدِ
pilgrim حَاجٌّ	and دَائِرَةُ ٱلْبَرِيدِ
— pilgrimage حَجٌّ	pretty جَمِيلٌ
pistol مُسَدَّسٌ	pupil تِلْمِيذٌ
to play لَعِبَ	— plural : تَلَامِيذُ
— Imperfect : يَلْعَبُ	to put وَضَعَ
to plough حَرَثَ	— Imperfect : يَضَعُ

Q

quarter رُبْعٌ	queen مَلِكَةٌ
— plural : أَرْبَاعٌ	question سُؤَالٌ
— of a town حَارَةٌ	— plural : أَسْئِلَةٌ

R

to read قَرَأَ

— Imperfect يَقْرَأُ

red أَحْمَرُ

— feminine حَمْرَاءُ

— plural حُمْرٌ

restaurant مَطْعَمٌ

— plural مَطَاعِمُ

to return رَجَعَ

— Imperfect يَرْجِعُ

rich غَنِيٌّ

— richer أَغْنَى

to ride رَكِبَ

— Imperfect يَرْكَبُ

— Imperative إِرْكَبْ

river نَهْرٌ

— plural بُهُورٌ ، أَنْهُرٌ

room غُرْفَةٌ

— plural غُرَفٌ

S

— Imperfect يَقُولُ

school مَدْرَسَةٌ

— plural مَدَارِسُ

sea بَحْرٌ

— plural بِحَارٌ and أَبْحُرٌ

second (1/60 minute) ثَانِيَةٌ

— plural ثَوَانٍ

— the second (2nd) أَلثَّانِي

Saddle سَرْجٌ

— plural سُرُوجٌ

sailor مَلَّاحٌ

— plural مَلَّاحُونَ

sand رَمْلٌ

Saturday يَوْمُ ٱلسَّبْتِ

to say قَالَ

— I said قُلْتُ

secret سِرٌّ	sick مَرِيضٌ
plural ـ أَسْرَارٌ	silk حَرِيرٌ
to see رَأَى	silver فِضَّةٌ
ـ I saw رَأَيْتُ	simple بَسِيطٌ
ـ Imperfect يَرَى	Sir سَيِّدٌ
to sell بَاعَ	ـ plural سَادَةٌ
ـ I sold بِعْتُ	sister أُخْتٌ
ـ Imperfect يَبِيعُ	ـ plural أَخَوَاتٌ
seven سَبْعَةٌ	six سِتَّةٌ
ـ feminine سَبْعٌ	ـ feminine سِتٌّ
ـ the seventh أَلسَّابِعُ	ـ the sixth أَلسَّادِسُ
ـ seventeen سَبْعَةَ عَشَرَ	ـ sixteen سِتَّةَ عَشَرَ
ـ feminine سَبْعَ عَشْرَةَ	ـ feminine سِتَّ عَشْرَةَ
ـ seventy سَبْعُونَ	ـ sixty سِتُّونَ
she هِيَ	small صَغِيرٌ
ـ she has لَهَا See also lesson 11 B.	ـ smaller أَصْغَرُ
shop دُكَّانٌ	son إِبْنٌ
ـ plural دَكَاكِينُ	ـ plural أَبْنَاءُ and بَنُونَ
short قَصِيرٌ	

sour	حَامِضٌ
to sow	زَرَعَ
— Imperfect	يَزْرَعُ
to stand	وَقَفَ
— Imperfect	يَقِفُ
— to stand up	قَامَ
— Imperfect	يَقُومُ
station	مَحَطَّةٌ
to steal	سَرَقَ
— Imperfect	يَسْرِقُ

straight	مُسْتَقِيمٌ
street	شَارِعٌ
— plural	شَوَارِعُ
stupid	أَحْمَقُ
sugar	سُكَّرٌ
sun	شَمْسٌ
Sunday	يَوْمُ ٱلْأَحَدِ
sweet	حُلْوٌ
sword	سَيْفٌ
— plural	سُيُوفٌ

T

table	مَائِدَةٌ
— plural	مَوَائِدُ
tailor	خَيَّاطٌ
— plural	خَيَّاطُونَ
to take	أَخَذَ
— Imperfect	يَأْخُذُ
— Imperative	خُذْ
teacher	مُعَلِّمٌ

— plural	مُعَلِّمُونَ
ten	عَشَرَةٌ
— feminine	عَشْرٌ
— the tenth	ٱلْعَاشِرُ
tent	خَيْمَةٌ
— plural	خِيَامٌ
than (see page 118. Note)	مِنْ
that	ذٰلِكَ

— feminine تِلْكَ	— imperfect يَظُنُّ
— that ox ذَلِكَ ٱلثَّوْرُ	this هٰذَا
— that cow تِلْكَ ٱلْبَقَرَةُ	— feminine هٰذِهِ
thee كَ (كِ fem) See lesson 17	— this ox هٰذَا ٱلثَّوْرُ
their هُمْ (suffix) See lesson 8 and lesson 48 A. B.	— this cow هٰذِهِ ٱلْبَقَرَةُ
— feminine هُنَّ (suffix)	thou أَنْتَ
them هُمْ (suffix) See lesson 17	— feminine أَنْتِ
— feminine هُنَّ (suffix)	— thou hast لَكَ
then ثُمَّ	— fem لَكِ See also lesson 11 B.
there هُنَاكَ	thousand أَلْفٌ
these هٰؤُلَاءِ	— plural أُلُوفٌ and آلَافٌ
they هُمْ	three ثَلْثَةٌ and ثَلَاثَةٌ
— feminine هُنَّ	— fem. ثَلْثٌ and ثَلَاثٌ
— they have لَهُمْ	— the third ٱلثَّالِثُ
— fem. لَهُنَّ See also lesson 11 B.	— thirteen ثَلَاثَةَ عَشَرَ
thief سَارِقٌ	— fem. ثَلَاثَ عَشَرَةَ
thing شَيْءٌ	— thirty ثَلَاثُونَ
— plural أَشْيَاءُ	thursday يَوْمُ ٱلْخَمِيسِ
to think (believe) ظَنَّ	thy كَ (suffix) See lesson 8 and lesson 48. A. B.

- feminine : كِ (suffix)	tree شَجَرَةٌ
ime وَقْتٌ	tribe قَبِيلَةٌ
- plural : أَوْقَاتٌ	— plural : قَبَائِلُ
ired تَعْبَانُ	Tuesday يَوْمُ ٱلثَّلَاثَاءِ
إِلَى o	twelve إِثْنَا عَشَرَ
o-day أَلْيَوْمَ	— feminine : إِثْنَتَا عَشَرَةَ
o-morrow غَدًا	twenty عِشْرُونَ
oo أَيْضاً	twice مَرَّتَانِ
ooth سِنٌّ	two إِثْنَانِ
- plural : أَسْنَانٌ	— feminine : إِثْنَتَانِ — See also lesson 32

U

ncle عَمٌّ (on the father's side)	— imperfect : يَفْهَمُ
خَالٌ (on the mother's side)	until حَتَّى ؛ إِلَى أَنْ
nder تَحْتَ	upon فَوْقَ ؛ عَلَى
understand فَهِمَ	us نَا (suffix) See lesson 17

V

ery جِدًّا	village قَرْيَةٌ
est صَدْرِيَّةٌ	— plural : قُرًى

vineyard	كَرْمٌ	vocabulary	قَامُوسٌ
— plural :	كُرُومٌ	— plural :	قَوَامِيسُ
to visit	زَارَ	voice	صَوْتٌ
— I visited	زُرْتُ	— plural :	أَصْوَاتٌ
— imperfect :	يَزُورُ	volume	مُجَلَّدٌ

W

war	حَرْبٌ	— plural :	أَسَابِيعُ
— plural :	حُرُوبٌ	to weep	بَكَى
watchman	حَارِسٌ	— imperfect :	يَبْكِي
water	مَاءٌ	weighty	ثَقِيلٌ
— plural :	مِيَاهٌ	west	غَرْبٌ
way	طَرِيقٌ	what ?	مَاذَا ، مَا
— plural :	طُرُقٌ	when ?	مَتَى
we	نَحْنُ	where ?	أَيْنَ
— we have	لَنَا See also lesson 11 B.	which	أَلَّذِي
Wednesday	يَوْمُ ٱلْأَرْبَعَاءِ	— feminine :	أَلَّتِي
week	جُمْعَةٌ ، أُسْبُوعٌ	— plural :	أَلَّذِينَ

wire	سِلْكٌ
— plural :	سُلُوكٌ ، أَسْلَاكٌ
— wireless	لَا سِلْكِيٌّ
with	بِ ، مَعَ
wolf	ذِئْبٌ
— plural :	ذِئَابٌ
woman	إِمْرَأَةٌ
— plural :	نِسَاءٌ
wonderful	عَجِيبٌ
woodcutter	حَطَّابٌ
wool	صُوفٌ
to write	كَتَبَ
— imperfect :	يَكْتُبُ

Y

yesterday	أَلْبَارِحَةَ ، أَلْبَارِحَ
you — feminine :	أَنْتُنَّ — أَنْتُمْ
— you (masc.) have	لَكُمْ

white	أَبْيَضُ
fem.	بَيْضَاءُ
plural :	بِيضٌ
who?	مَنْ
why?	لِمَاذَا
wide	وَاسِعٌ ، عَرِيضٌ
wife (consort)	زَوْجَةٌ
wind	رِيحٌ
plural :	رِيَاحٌ
window	شُبَّاكٌ
plural :	شَبَابِيكُ
wine	خَمْرٌ
winter	شِتَاءٌ
year	سَنَةٌ
plural :	سَنَوَاتٌ ، سِنُونَ
yes	نَعَمْ

— you (fem.) have تَكُنّ See
also lesson 11 B.

— YOU in abjective case كُمْ (suffix)

— fem. كُنّ (suffix). See lesson 17

young صَغِيرُ ٱلسِّنّ

— younger than أَصْغَرُ سِنًّا مِنْ

— your كُمْ (suffix) See lesson 8 a
lesson 48 A, B

— feminine : كُنّ (suffix)

KEY

to the

Arabic Language and Grammar

VOLUME ONE

by

Dr. JOCHANAN KAPLIWATZKY

RUBIN MASS / JERUSALEM

Note 1: In this key a translation is given only of the texts for the conversation-lessons in the book "Arabic Language and Grammar". The texts of the stories in the above book are composed of the matter in the preceding conversation-lessons and therefore no translation of it is necessary here.

Note 2: The English translation here of the Arabic text in the book "Arabic Language and Grammar" is, as far as possible, a litt era one. care being taken especially to the Arabic original in order to facilitate the understanding of the structure of the Arabic sentences for the English beginner. For the same reason the second person singular (thou, thee, thy) is used in the key as well as in the book.

Fifth Lesson

1. I have a house and thou (m.) hast a house   2. We have a large house   3. He has a big dog and she has a big dog 4. They (m.) have a fat dog and they (f.) have a fat dog 5. We have a large garden and they (m.) have a large vineyard 6. She has a vineyard and he has a garden 7. Thou (m.) hast a large garden and a large vineyard. 8. A vineyard and a garden 9. A house and a vineyard   10. She has a big book and I have a big book   11. You (m.) have a book and they (m.) have a book 12. We have a fat ox and you (f.) have a fat ox   13. He has an ox and thou (m.) hast an ox and a dog.

١. لَنَا كَلْبٌ وَلَهُمْ كَلْبٌ ٢. لَهُ بَيْتٌ كَبِيرٌ وَلَهَا
بُسْتَانٌ كَبِيرٌ ٣. لَهُمْ ثَوْرٌ سَمِينٌ وَكَلْبٌ سَمِينٌ ٤. لَهُمْ
كَرْمٌ كَبِيرٌ وَلَهُنَّ بَيْتٌ كَبِيرٌ ٥. لَكِ كِتَابٌ وَلَنَا
كِتَابٌ ٦. لَهَا كِتَابٌ كَبِيرٌ وَلَهُنَّ كِتَابٌ كَبِيرٌ
٧. لَهُنَّ كَلْبٌ سَمِينٌ وَلِي ثَوْرٌ سَمِينٌ.

Seventh Lesson

1. I have a father and a mother and he has a father and a mother   2. A big door and a big window   3. We have a big door and they (m.) have a big window   4 She has a big and a fat cock and they (f.) have a big and a fat cock 5. You (m.) have a fat ox and a big dog   6. You (f.) have a house and a garden and she has a large vineyard 7. I and thou (m.)   8. Thou (m.) and he   9. He is big and fat and thou (m.) art big and fat   10. I have a big and fat elephant and he has a fat ox   11. She has a copy-book and a book and thou (f.) hast a copy-book and a book   12. An elephant and an ox. A house and a garden.

١. بَابٌ كَبِيرٌ وَشُبَّاكٌ كَبِيرٌ ٢. لَكِ فِيلٌ سَمِينٌ
وَلَنَا ثَوْرٌ كَبِيرٌ وَسَمِينٌ ٣. لِي دَفْتَرٌ وَكِتَابٌ وَلَهُ

كِتَابٌ ٤. لَهَا دِيكٌ سَمِينٌ ٥. لَنَا كَلْبٌ وَلَكِنْ
كَلْبٌ ٦. أَبٌ وَأُمٌّ ٧. أَنَا وَهُوَ. هُوَ وَأَنْتَ ٨. هُوَ
سَمِينٌ ٩. أَنْتَ سَمِينٌ وَكَبِيرٌ ١٠. لَكُمْ أَبٌ وَأُمٌّ
وَلَنَا أَبٌ وَأُمٌّ.

Ninth Lesson

1. I have a hare and thou (m.) hast a hare   2. Thy (m.) hare is bigger than my hare   3. He has a dog and I have a dog   4. His dog is fatter than my dog   5 Salim is a big boy   6. Shakir is a big pupil   7. Salim is bigger than my pupil   8. Shakir is bigger than my boy   9. Where is thy (m.) ox ? — My ox is in my garden   10. Thy (m.) book is bigger than my book   11. Her vineyard is bigger than my vineyard   12. His ox is bigger and fatter than my ox   13. Thy (m.) ox and thy (m.) dog are in my garden   14. Where is thy (m.) pupil ?— My pupil is in my vineyard   15. His house is bigger than my house   16. Where is my hare ?— Thy (m.) hare is in my vineyard.

١. كَلْبُهُ أَسْمَنُ مِنْ كَلْبِي ٢. أَيْنَ ثَوْرُهُمْ؟ -
ثَوْرُهُمْ فِي بُسْتَانِي ٣. دِيكُهَا أَسْمَنُ مِنْ دِيكِي ٤. أَرْنَبُكَ
فِي بُسْتَانِي ٥. وَلَدُهُ أَكْبَرُ مِنْ وَلَدِي ٦. أَيْنَ تِلْمِيذِي
وَتِلْمِيذُكَ؟ - تِلْمِيذِي وَتِلْمِيذُكَ فِي كَرْمِي ٧. لِي ثَوْرٌ
وَلَهَا ثَوْرٌ. ثَوْرُهَا أَكْبَرُ وَأَسْمَنُ مِنْ ثَوْرِي ٨. أَيْنَ
كَلْبُنَا؟ - كَلْبُكُمْ فِي بَيْتِي

Twelfth Lesson

1. What is this ?— This is an ass   2. This is my ass
3. This is thy (m.) dog   4. My ass ate and thy (m.) ass did
not eat   5. I ate and thou (m.) didst not eat   6. Who has
written and who has drawn ? — Salim has written and I have
drawn 7. I have a brother and a sister and he has a brother
and a sister   8. Shakir is bigger than my brother   9. I have
a camel and thou (m.) hast a camel. Thy (m.) camel is bigger
and fatter than my camel 10. Who went out of my garden ?
— My brother went out from there 11. Who has eaten in my
garden ? — My father has eaten there   12. My brother has
written here and my sister has written there 13. My camel has
eaten here and thy (m.) camel has eaten there   14. They (m.)
have written and did not draw   15. They (f.) have drawn and
did not write   16. We went out of my garden and you (m.)
did not go out from there 17. They (m.) have drawn and you
(f.) did not draw 18. We and you (m.). They (m.) and you (f.).
I and they (f.). Thou (m.) and he. She and thou (f.)   19. We
have written and did not draw. You (m·) have drawn and did
not write. They (m.) have written and did not draw.

١. أَنَا أَكَلْتُ وَأَنْتِ مَا أَكَلْتِ ٢. هُمْ كَتَبُوا
وَنَحْنُ رَسَمْنَا ٣. أَبِي خَرَجَ مِنْ بُسْتَانِي ٤. أُمِّي خَرَجَتْ مِنْ
كَرْمِي ٥. نَحْنُ كَتَبْنَا وَهُوَ مَا كَتَبَ ٦. لِتِلْمِيذِي أَخٌ
وَأُخْتٌ وَلَكِ أَخٌ ٧. جَمَلُكَ أَكَلَ وَحِمَارِي مَا أَكَلَ ٨. مَا
هٰذَا ؟— هٰذَا جَمَلٌ ٩. كَلْبُكُمْ أَكْبَرُ وَأَسْمَنُ مِنْ كَلْبِي
١٠. أَكَلْنَا فِي بُسْتَانِي ١١. هُوَ أَكَلَ وَهِيَ مَا أَكَلَتْ
١٢. أُخْتِي كَتَبَتْ وَأَنْتُنَّ مَا كَتَبْتُنَّ ١٣. أَخُوكُمْ
خَرَجَ مِنْ كَرْمِي ١٤. نَحْنُ أَكَلْنَا وَهِيَ مَا أَكَلَتْ .

Fourteenth Lesson

1. My vineyard is far and thy (m.) vineyard is near from here **2.** His house is near from here and his garden is far from here **3.** Who has read and who has written?—My sister has read and I have written **4.** What did thy (m.) sister read?— My sister read my book **5.** My dog is black and thy (m.) dog is red **6,** I have blue ink and thou (m.) hast black ink **7.** My copy-book is heavy and thy (m.) copy-book is light **8.** My brother has read my newspaper and my neighbour has written in my copy-book **9.** They (f.) have read and they (m.) have written **10.** We have written and you (m.) have read **11.** My garden is far from here and thy (m.) garden is farther than it **12.** My vineyard is near from here and his vineyard is farther than it **13.** My ink is blue and thy (m.) ink is black **14.** My cock is heavy and his cock is light **15.** He has read my newspaper and she did not read.

١. أُخْتُكَ كَتَبَتْ وَأَنَا قَرَأْتُ ٢. أَيْنَ جَارُكَ ؟— هُوَ فِي كَرْمِي ٣. حِبْرُهَا أَسْوَدُ وَحِبْرُهُ أَزْرَقُ ٤. بُسْتَانُهُنَّ أَقْرَبُ مِنْ كَرْمِي ٥. دِيكُكَ أَثْقَلُ مِنْ دِيكِي ٦. مَا قَرَأَ ؟— هُوَ قَرَأَ جَرِيدَتِي ٧. بَيْتُكُمْ أَقْرَبُ مِنْ بَيْتِي ٨. مَنْ قَرَأَ وَمَنْ كَتَبَ ؟— أَنَا كَتَبْتُ وَجَارِي قَرَأَ ٩. نَحْنُ قَرَأْنَا وَهُمْ مَا قَرَؤُوا ١٠. هِيَ كَتَبَتْ وَأُخْتُهَا مَا كَتَبَتْ ١١. هِيَ أَكَلَتْ وَهُوَ مَا أَكَلَ ١٢. بَيْتُهُ أَكْبَرُ مِنْ بَيْتِي ١٣. دَفْتَرُهُ أَثْقَلُ مِنْ دَفْتَرِي ١٤. أَيْنَ كَلْبُكُمْ ؟— كَلْبِي فِي بُسْتَانِي

Fifteenth Lesson

1. Who has drunk and who has eaten :— My brother has drunk and I have eaten   2. They (m.) ate and did not drink and they (f.) drank and did not eat   3. My hare has drunk and thy (f.) hare has not drunk   4. His hare is fatter than my hare   5. My brother entered my vineyard and thy (m.) neighbour went out of it   6 I have a fat lamb and she has a fat lamb   7. His lamb is big and my lamb is bigger (than it)   8. Thou (m.) art bigger than my brother and I am bigger than thee (m.)   9. Thy (f.) pupil is big and her pupil is bigger (than he)   10. Who went out of my garden?— My grand-father went out of it   11. My grand-mother entered my garden and went out of it   12. Where is thy (m.) grand-father and thy grand-mother ?— My grand-father and my grand-mother are in my vineyard   13. My father and my grand-mother are in my garden and my mother and grand-mother are in my vineyard.

١. جَدُّكَ كَتَبَ وَأَبِي قَرَأَ   ٢. خَرُوفُكُمْ أَسْمَنُ مِنْ خَرُوفِي   ٣. أَيْنَ أُمُّنَا ؟— أُمُّكُنَّ فِي كَرْمِي   ٤. تِلْمِيذُكِ كَبِيرٌ وَتِلْمِيذِي أَكْبَرُ مِنْهُ   ٥. جَدَّتُهُ دَخَلَتْ بُسْتَانِي   ٦. جَمَلِي شَرِبَ وَجَمَلُهَا مَا شَرِبَ   ٧. هُمْ شَرِبُوا وَنَحْنُ مَا شَرِبْنَا   ٨. هُوَ خَرَجَ مِنْ بَيْتِي   ٩. بَيْتِي أَقْرَبُ مِنْ بَيْتِهِ   ١٠. أُخْتِي شَرِبَتْ وَأُخْتُهُ مَا شَرِبَتْ   ١١. فِيلُهَا أَكْبَرُ مِنْ فِيلِي

Eighteenth Lesson

1. Where did Ibrahim find my horse ?— He found it in my garden   2. Where did Ahmad find my cow ?— he found it in my vineyard   3. Who has beaten my brother ?— Thy (m.) neighbour has beaten him   4. Who found you (m.) in my garden ? — Thy (m.) neighbour found us there   5. Who

has beaten you (m.) ? — Thy (m.) neighbour has beaten us
6. Who has eaten my bread ? — We have eaten it   7. Who
has drunk my milk ?— We have drunk it   8. Who has beaten
thee (m.)?— Thy (m.) neighbour has beaten me   9. Who has
broken my cup ?— Thy (m.) sister has broken it   10. Who has
beaten my ass ?— Thy (m.) pupil has beaten it 11. My brother
did not break my cup. My sister has broken it   12. My sister
has drunk my milk and my brother did not drink it   13. Who
has beaten my camel ?— Ahmad has beaten it   14. Your (m.)
horse is bigger and fatter than my horse   15. I have black
ink and he has green ink   16. She has a black dog and you
(m.) have a white dog   17. I have a horse and an ass and
you (m.) have an ox and a camel 18. Thy (m.) cup is bigger
than my cup.

١. مَنْ وَجَدَ كِتَابِي ؟— أُخْتِي وَجَدَتْهُ   ٢. مَنْ
ضَرَبَ تِلْمِيذِي ؟—جَارُنَا ضَرَبَهُ   ٣. مَنْ كَسَرَ فِنْجَانِي؟
أُخْتُهُمْ كَسَرَتْهُ   ٤. حِبْرُكُنَّ أَسْوَدُ وَحِبْرُنَا أَزْرَقُ
٥. حِبْرُهَا أَخْضَرُ وَحِبْرُهُ أَحْمَرُ   ٦. إِبْرَهِيمُ أَكْبَرُ مِنْ
أَخِي   ٧. أَحْمَدُ كَسَرَ فِنْجَانِي   ٨. لِي حِمَارٌ وَلَهَا حِمَارٌ
حِمَارُهَا أَسْمَنُ مِنْ حِمَارِي   ٩. حِصَانُهُ كَبِيرٌ وَحِصَانُكَ
أَكْبَرُ مِنْهُ   ١١. كَلْبُكُمْ أَسْوَدُ وَ كَلْبُهُنَّ أَبْيَضُ
١٢. أَخُوهَا ضَرَبَ ثَوْرِي   ١٣. أَيْنَ وَجَدَ فِنْجَانِي ؟—
هُوَ وَجَدَهُ فِي كَرْمِي   ١٤. (نَحْنُ) وَجَدْنَاهَا. (هِيَ)
وَجَدَتْهُ. (أَنَا) وَجَدْتُهَا. (أَنْتَ) وَجَدْتَنِي .

Twentieth Lesson

1. Who will write and who will draw? — My mother will write and my sister will draw 2. They (m.) have written and you (m.) did not write. 3. They (m.) will write (write) and you (m.) will not write (do not write). 4. They (f.) have drunk and you (f.) did not drink 5. They (f.) will drink (drink) and you (f.) will (do) not drink 6. My cow drinks now and thy (m.) cow does not drink 7. Where does fatima write? — She writes in my copy-book 8. Salih has now written and I did not write 9. Where didst thou (m.) leave my ox? — I left it in my garden. 10. Shakir left my book in my school 11. Who has opened my book? — My pupil has opened it 12. I have a table and a chair and thou (m.) hast a table and a bench 13. Thy (m.) table is bigger than my table 14. Where is my brother Ahmad? — He is in my school 15. My sister Fatima is bigger than I and I am bigger than thee (f.) 18. Who opened my book? — I did not open it. Thy (m.) pupil Shakir opened it 19. She will go (goes) out and thou (f.) wilt not (dost not) go out 20. Thou (m.) wilt draw and he will not draw 21. Ibrahim writes and Fatima does not write 22. You (m.) went out of my garden and they (m.) do (will) not go out of it.

١. أَخُوكَ كَتَبَ وَنَحْنُ مَا كَتَبْنَا ٢. نَحْنُ نَكْتُبُ وَأَنْتُمْ لَا تَكْتُبُونَ ٣. مَائِدَتُكَ أَكْبَرُ مِنْ مَائِدَتِي ٤. لِي كُرْسِيٌّ وَبَنْكُ وَلَهَا مَائِدَةٌ وَكُرْسِيٌّ ٥. أَيْنَ كَتَبَ سَلِيمٌ؟ ـ هُوَ كَتَبَ فِي كَرْمِي ٦. ثَوْرُهُ أَسْوَدُ وَثَوْرُهَا أَبْيَضُ ٧. تِلْمِيذٌ كُمْ كَسَرَ كُرْسِيّ ٨. حِصَانُكَ أَكْبَرُ وَأَسْمَنُ مِنْ حِصَانِي ٩. أَيْنَ أَخُوهَا؟ ـ هُوَ فِي مَدْرَسَتِي ١٠. هُمْ يَكْتُبُونَ وَهُوَ لَا يَكْتُبُ ١١. أُخْتُنَا شَرِبَتْ وَأُخْتُكَ مَا شَرِبَتْ ١٢. أَيْنَ خَرُوفُهُ؟ ـ خَرُوفُهُ فِي بُسْتَانِي ١٣. أَنَا كَتَبْتُ وَجَدِّي مَا كَتَبَ

١٤. بَيْتُكُنَّ أَقْرَبُ مِنْ بَيْتِي. ١٥. لَنَا ثَوْرٌ وَحِمَارٌ وَلَهُ

جَمَلٌ وَبَقَرَةٌ. ١٦. لَهَا أُخْتٌ وَلِي أُخْتٌ وَأَخٌ.

Twenty-second Lesson

1. Where art thou (m.) going, my brother ?— I am going (I go,, or I shall go) to my school   2. Where is thy (m.) book ? —My book is on my table   3. My sister went out of my room and my brother did not go out from there   4. My brother returned from Jaffa and my father will return to-morrow from there   5. My teacher went with my grand-father to my school   6. Who went out with thee (m.) from my room?—Thy (m.) teacher went out with me from there   7. I have a big dog and thou (m.) hast a small dog. Thy (m.) dog is smaller than my dog   8. My brother is smaller than I and I am smaller than thou (m.)   9. My neighbour is very poor and thy (m.) neighbour is very rich   10. Thy (m.) camel is smaller than my camel and thy (m.) ass is bigger than my ass   11. Ahmad is very poor and Salim is poorer than he   12. Ibrahim is very rich and Shakir is richer than he.

١. أَيْنَ جَرِيدَتِي ؟ — جَرِيدَتُكَ عَلَى مَائِدَتِي. ٢. حِصَانُهُ

أَصْغَرُ مِنْ حِصَانِي. ٣. ثَوْرُهَا كَبِيرٌ جِدًّا. ٤. إِبْرَاهِيمُ

أَغْنَى مِنْ جَارِي. ٥. جَارُهُ غَنِيٌّ وَجَارُنَا فَقِيرٌ. ٦. يَا سَلِيمُ

أَيْنَ كِتَابِي ؟ — كِتَابُكَ فِي غُرْفَتِي. ٧. بُسْتَانُكُمْ أَصْغَرُ

مِنْ بُسْتَانِي. بُسْتَانِي كَبِيرٌ جِدًّا. ٨. أَنْتَ أَكْبَرُ مِنْ

أَخِي. ٩. أَيْنَ جَدِّي ؟ — هُوَ فِي غُرْفَتِي. ١٠. جَدُّكُمْ

أَغْنَى مِنْ جَدِّي.

Twenty-fourth Lesson

1. This camel is small. It is smaller than my camel
2. This ass is cheap and that ass is cheaper than it **3.** That
tailor is poor. He is poorer than my neighbour **4.** Who was
in my room to-day ? — Zayd was there and the baker too was
there **5.** The barber was in Jaffa to-day and the blacksmith
also was there. **6.** Thy (m.) sister was in my garden and Fatima
also was there **7.** My mother was in Jaffa to-day and my sister
also was there **8.** Where is the new book ?— The new book is
on my table in my room **9.** When did Zayd return from Jaffa
and when did the barber return ?— Zayd returned from Jaffa to-
day and the barber also returned to-day **10.** What is this ?—
This is a dog **11.** This dog is bigger and fatter than my dog
12. This new house is larger than my house and that house is
smaller than it **13.** This elephant is big and that elephant is
bigger than it **14.** When didst thou (m.) return from Jaffa ?
—I returned from there to-day **15.** Thy (m.) grand-father was
in my vineyard and in my garden to-day **16.** Where is the
big dog and where is the ass ?— The big dog is in my garden
and the ass also is in my garden.

١. كِتَابُكَ أَرْخَصُ مِنْ كِتَابِي ٢. هٰذَا الْجَمَلُ
كَبِيرٌ وَذٰلِكَ الْجَمَلُ صَغِيرٌ ٣. هٰذَا الْخَيَّاطُ غَنِيٌّ
وَذٰلِكَ الْخَبَّازُ فَقِيرٌ ٤. اَلْحَلَّاقُ كَانَ فِي يَافَا وَالْحَدَّادُ
أَيْضًا كَانَ هُنَاكَ ٥. هٰذَا الْبَيْتُ الْجَدِيدُ أَكْبَرُ مِنْ
بَيْتِي ٦. ذٰلِكَ الْكِتَابُ الْجَدِيدُ أَرْخَصُ مِنْ كِتَابِي
الْجَدِيدِ ٧. مَتَى رَجَعْتَ مِنْ يَافَا ؟— أَنَا رَجَعْتُ الْيَوْمَ
مِنْ هُنَاكَ ٨. أَيْنَ الْخَيَّاطُ ؟— هُوَ فِي غُرْفَتِي ٩. هٰذَا
اَلْكَلْبُ أَكْبَرُ وَأَسْمَنُ مِنْ كَلْبِي ١١. بُسْتَانٌ كَبِيرٌ
اَلْبُسْتَانُ الْكَبِيرُ. هٰذَا الْبُسْتَانُ الْكَبِيرُ. هٰذَا الْبُسْتَانُ

كَبِيرٌ. ذَلِكَ ٱلْبُسْتَانُ. ذَلِكَ ٱلْبُسْتَانُ ٱلْكَبِيرُ.

ذَلِكَ ٱلْبُسْتَانُ كَبِيرٌ.

Twenty-sixth Lesson

1. Who opened the big door ?— I opened it 2. What hast thou (m.) eaten to-day ?— I have eaten bread and meat to-day 3 The dog of the neighbour is fatter than the dog of the barber 4. Where is the book of the director of the school ?— His book is on the table in the room of the grand-father 5. The grand-father of the neighbour was in the vineyard of my brother to-day 6. The neighbour of the tailor is poor. He is poorer than the neighbour of the blacksmith 7. Who visited thee (m.) in the school to-day ?— The teacher of Muhammad visited me there 8. What is thy (m.) name and what is the name of thy (m.) sister ?— My name is Isma'il and the name of my sister is Fatima 9. Thy (m.) sister visited the sister of the teacher to-day 10. Where is the son of the blacksmith ?— His son is in the house of the baker 11. Where is the dog of the uncle (on the mother's side) ? — The dog of the uncle is under the table 12. The house of the aunt (on the mother's side) and her vineyard 13. My uncle (on the father's side) has visited thy (m.) uncle in the new house to-day 14. My aunt (on the father's side) was in the vineyard of my grand-mother to-day 15. The big son of the teacher was in Jaffa to-day 16. Who drank the milk ? — I did not drink it. My brother Ibrahim drank it 17. My uncle (on the mother's side) visited the uncle of the neighbour in Jaffa 18. What is the name of the uncle (on the mother's side) ? — The name of the uncle is Isma'il 19. The name of my brother is Ibrahim and the name of my sister is Hind 20. This new house is larger than my house.

١. هَذَا ٱلْكَلْبُ كَبِيرٌ. هُوَ أَكْبَرُ مِنْ ذَلِكَ ٱلْكَلْبِ

٢. لِي حِمَارٌ وَلَهُ حِصَانٌ ٣ اَلْحِصَانُ أَكْبَرُ مِنَ ٱلْحِمَارِ

وَٱلْجَمَلُ أَكْبَرُ مِنَ ٱلْحِصَانِ ٤. أَيْنَ مُدِيرُ ٱلْمَدْرَسَةِ ؟—

هُوَ فِي غُرْفَةِ ٱلْجَدِّ ٥. مَا ٱسْمُكَ ؟— إِسْمِي سُلَيْمَانُ

٦. أَكَلْتُ خُبْزاً وَلَحْماً وَهِيَ شَرِبَتْ حَلِيباً ٧. هٰذَا
الْجَمَلُ أَكْبَرُ وَأَسْمَنُ مِنْ ذٰلِكَ الْجَمَلِ ٨. الْحَلَّاقُ
أَفْقَرُ مِنَ الْحَدَّادِ ٩. الْمُعَلِّمُ فِي غُرْفَةِ الْمُدِيرِ
١٠. الْحَدَّادُ فِي الْبَيْتِ الْجَدِيدِ ١١. هٰذَا الْفِيلُ كَبِيرٌ.
هُوَ أَكْبَرُ مِنْ فِيلِي ١٢. أَيْنَ الْخَيَّاطُ ؟ - هُوَ فِي
بَيْتِ الْخَبَّازِ ١٣. أَيْنَ الْكِتَابُ الْجَدِيدُ ؟ - الْكِتَابُ
الْجَدِيدُ عَلَى الْمَائِدَةِ .

Twenty-seventh Lesson

1. The hare is a small animal   2. My brother was in the park of the animals (zoo) to-day and my father will be there to-morrow   3. What has thy (m.) brother seen in the zoo ? — My brother has seen there a big lion in a big cage 4. Hast thou (m.) written to-day ?— Yes, I have written to-day 5. Hast thou (m.) opened the gate of the vineyard ?— No, I have not opened it. 6. Will thy (m.) brother be at school to-morrow? — Yes, he will be there to-morrow   7. What didst thou (m.) ask the baker and what did he answer ? — I asked him when he was in the house of the uncle (on the mother's side) and he answered that he was there to-day   8. I have a friend and his name is Salim 9. My father rode in a boat on sea and thy (m.) father will ride in a boat to-morrow 10. My brother rode an ass and thy (m.) brother rode a horse   11. The mariner died in the house of my friend   12. Who saw the brother of the mariner ? — The father of my friend saw the brother of the mariner   13. My grand-father visited the father of the teacher in Jaffa   14. The name of the father of the teacher is Tawfiq and the name of the brother of the director is Zayd.

١. أَيْنَ أَخُو الْمُدِيرِ ؟ - هُوَ فِي هٰذَا الْبُسْتَانِ. ٢. أَنَا
فَتَحْتُ بَابَ الْغُرْفَةِ ٣. أَيْنَ صَدِيقِي ؟ - صَدِيقُكَ فِي

غُرْفَةِ الْجَدِّ ٤. أَبُوهُمْ كَانَ الْيَوْمَ فِي الْمَدْرَسَةِ ٥. أَبُوهَا رَكِبَ حِمَارًا وَأَخُوهَا رَكِبَ حِصَانًا ٦. خَالِي زَارَ أَبَا الْمُعَلِّمِ ٧. مَنْ رَأَى أَخَا الْخَيَّاطِ ؟— أَخُو الْحَدَّادِ رَأَى أَخَا الْخَيَّاطِ ٨. الْأَسَدُ الْكَبِيرُ فِي قَفَصٍ كَبِيرٍ ٩. هَلْ كَتَبَ الْيَوْمَ ؟— نَعَمْ هُوَ كَتَبَ ١٠. أَفَتَحَ بَابَ الْغُرْفَةِ ؟— نَعَمْ هُوَ فَتَحَهُ

Twenty-ninth Lesson

1. This copy-book is big and that copy-book is small
2. This fox is bigger than my fox   3. Who opened the small
window ?— I opened the small window   4. Where dost thou
(m.) go, my uncle ?— I go to the new shop   5. My sister was
in the new market 6. I went to the market in the morning and
returned from there in the evening 7. The father of Salim was
at school in the forenoon 8. What hast thou (m.) drunk in the
forenoon and what hast thou (m.) drunk in the after-noon ? — In
the forenoon I drank a cup of milk and in the after-noon I drank
a cup of coffee   9. This pupil is bigger than the pupil of my
brother 10. Where is the fat ox ?—The fat ox is in the garden
of the carpenter 11. Shakir saw a pretty bird on the tree 12. My
brother drank a cup of coffee and my uncle (on the father's side)
drank milk   13. Where is the bird of Muhammad ?— His bird
is in a small cage 14. I have a fox and a hare and thou (m.)
hast a dog and a lamb   15. Where is the little bird ?— The
little bird is on the tree   16. Where is the new chair ?— The
new chair is under the tree.

١. شَرِبْتُ فِنْجَانَ قَهْوَةٍ وَأُخْتِي شَرِبَتْ حَلِيبًا ٢. أَخِي كَانَ فِي الدُّكَّانِ الْجَدِيدِ ٣. جَدِّي كَانَ فِي الْمَدْرَسَةِ وَرَجَعَ مِنْ هُنَاكَ بَعْدَ الظُّهْرِ ٤. أُخْتُهَا

كَانَتْ فِي السُّوقِ صَبَاحًا ٥. أَيْنَ الْعُصْفُورُ الصَّغِيرُ؟

ـ هُوَ عَلَى الشَّجَرَةِ فِي الْبُسْتَانِ ٦. لِي ثَعْلَبٌ وَلَهُ ثَعْلَبٌ

٧. هَذَا الثَّعْلَبُ أَسْمَنُ مِنْ ذَلِكَ الثَّعْلَبِ ٨. هَذَا

الثَّوْرُ أَكْبَرُ مِنْ ذَلِكَ الثَّوْرِ ٩. أَيْنَ تِلْمِيذُ كُمْ؟ ـ

هُوَ فِي غُرْفَةِ النَّجِدِّ ١٠. أَيْنَ بَيْتُ الْخَيَّاطِ؟ ـ بَيْتُ

الْخَيَّاطِ فِي السُّوقِ ١١. أَيْنَ النَّجَّارُ؟ ـ النَّجَّارُ فِي

بُسْتَانِ الْخَبَّازِ ١٢. هَذَا النَّجَّارُ أَفْقَرُ مِنْ ذَلِكَ النَّجَّارِ

١٣. هَذَا الْعُصْفُورُ أَكْبَرُ مِنْ ذَلِكَ الْعُصْفُورِ ١٤. أَخِي

كَانَ فِي الْمَدْرَسَةِ صَبَاحًا وَأُخْتِي كَانَتْ هُنَاكَ بَعْدَ الظُّهْرِ

Thirty-first Lesson

1. When did thy (m.) brother mount the mount and when did he descend from it?— My brother mounted the mount in the forenoon 2. What did thy (m.) brother eat and what did thy (m.) sister eat ?— My brother ate bread and a piece of meat and my sister ate bread and a piece of cheese 3. Where is the (she-)cat of my aunt (on the mother's side) ?—It is in the little room 4. My grand-mother has a (she-)cat and an ape. The ape is bigger than the (she-)cat. 5. This hand is clean and that hand is dirty 6. This foot is clean and that foot is dirty 7. Who has taken the newspaper of the teacher?— I do not know who has taken it 8. Dost thou (m.) know the brother of Salim?— No, I do not know him 9. Who raised this newspaper from the earth ?— I raised it 10. My brother found a nut on the earth and raised it 11. Salim raised this nut from the earth 12. Where is the newspaper of my brother ?—Ibrahim took it and put it on the big table 13. Where is my little brother ?— He is in the forest 14. Thy (m.) brother plays with my brother in the forest 15. Ahmad played with my brother in the forest.

١. هٰذِهِ ٱلْمَدْرَسَةُ صَغِيرَةٌ وَتِلْكَ ٱلْمَدْرَسَةُ كَبِيرَةٌ

٢. أَيْنَ هِرَّةُ ٱلْأُخْتِ ؟ - هِرَّتُهَا فِي تِلْكَ ٱلْغُرْفَةِ ٣. هٰذِهِ

ٱلْغُرْفَةُ كَبِيرَةٌ وَتِلْكَ ٱلْغُرْفَةُ صَغِيرَةٌ ٤. هَلْ يَعْرِفُ

أَخُوكَ أَيْنَ مُدِيرُ هٰذِهِ ٱلْمَدْرَسَةِ ؟ - لَا هُوَ لَا

يَعْرِفُ أَيْنَ هُوَ ٥. هٰذِهِ ٱلرَّجُلُ نَظِيفَةٌ وَتِلْكَ

ٱلرَّجُلُ وَسِخَةٌ ٦. غُرْفَةُ ٱلْأُخْتِ نَظِيفَةٌ وَغُرْفَةُ

ٱلْأَخِ وَسِخَةٌ ٧. هٰذِهِ ٱلْبَقَرَةُ سَمِينَةٌ ٨. ذٰلِكَ

ٱلْكَلْبُ أَكْبَرُ مِنْ هٰذَا ٱلْكَلْبِ ٩. تِلْكَ ٱلْبَقَرَةُ

كَبِيرَةٌ وَهٰذِهِ ٱلْبَقَرَةُ صَغِيرَةٌ ١٠. مَنْ كَانَ فِي هٰذِهِ

ٱلْغُرْفَةِ وَمَنْ كَانَ فِي تِلْكَ ٱلْغُرْفَةِ ؟ - أَخُوكَ كَانَ

فِي هٰذِهِ ٱلْغُرْفَةِ وَأَخُوهُ كَانَ فِي تِلْكَ ٱلْغُرْفَةِ

Thirty-third Lesson

1. I have two big oxen and thou (m.) hast two big cows
2. The two dogs of my brother are big and the two dogs of my grand-father are small   3. Thy (m.) two cows are small and his two cows are big   4. My brother divided the piece of the cheese in two parts. He ate the one (In Araiic : the first) part and my sister ate the other part 5. I bought two cows to-day, one cow before noon and one cow in the after-noon. The one (first) cow is small and the other is big   6. This tailor is old. He is older than that tailor   7. These two dogs are small and those two cows are big   8. The bread which thou (m.) hast bought in the new market is cheaper than the bread which I have bought in the shop   9. Who has split the nut which was on the table in my room and who has eaten its core ? — Salim

split it and ate its core   10. These two vineyards are bigger
than the two vineyards of my brother   11. These two newspapers are bigger than the two newspapers of Zayd 12. These
two asses are smaller than thy (m.) two asses 13. We have
two vineyards and you (m.) have two houses.

Thirty-fourth Lesson

1. Ibrahim divided the piece of the meat into two parts.
Then he put each of the two parts in a scale of the balance
2. The balance of my brother is bigger than the balance of thy
(m.) grand-father   3. What hast thou (m.) done with the sugar
which I have bought in the new market?—I first divided it into
two parts then I put each of the two parts on the table in my
room   4. My brother has two oxen and I have two fat cows
5. Thy (m.) father said to thy (m.) brother : draw for me
two automobiles and thy (m.) brother drew then two automobiles
6. My brother and my sister went to school in the forenoon
and returned from there in the after-noon   7. Where is my sister
and thy (m.) sister ? — They (dual) went to school   8. From
where did I and my brother return?— You (dual) have returned
from school   9. This book is cheap and that book is a
little cheaper than it   10· I drank a little from the milk and
ate a little from the bread and my brother ate and drank
more than I   11. The two new houses of my brother are
much larger than the two houses of Salim 12. The two sisters
of Salim have much written and read to-day   13. I have not
gone to school to-day because my father is ill   14. My
brother has not gone to school to-day because he is ill
15. What hast thou (m.) eaten in the forenoon? — I ate bread
and a piece of meat.

١. كَلْبَا أَخِي فِي بُسْتَانِ أُخْتِكَ ٢. اَلْأَرْنَبَانِ اَلْكَبِيرَانِ

فِي كَرْمِ اَلْعَمِّ .   ٣. لِي بَيْتَانِ وَلِأَبِي أَيْضًا بَيْتَانِ .

بَيْتَاهُ فِي اَلسُّوقِ اَلْجَدِيدِ   ٤. بَقَرَتَا جَدَّتِي أَسْمَنُ مِنْ

بَقَرَتَيِ اَلْخَيَّاطِ   ٥. أَيْنَ جَرِيدَتَا اَلْمُدِيرِ ؟ - هُمَا عَلَى

اَلْمَائِدَةِ فِي غُرْفَةِ اَلْأَبِ   ٦. بَيْتُ اَلْخَبَّازِ وَبُسْتَانُهُ

٧. ثَوْرَاهَا أَكْبَرُ مِنْ ثَوْرَيْهِ   ٨. كَلْبَا ٱلْخَيَّاطِ وَأَرْنَبَاهُ

٩. حِمَارَا خَالَتِي وَجَمَلَاهَا   ١٠. لَهُ حِمَارٌ وَاحِدٌ وَثَوْرَانِ

وَلَنَا حِمَارَانِ وَثَوْرٌ وَاحِدٌ

Thirty-sixth Lesson

١. أَخِي وَقَفَ بَيْنَ ٱلْجَدِّ وَٱلْأُخْتِ   ٢. مَا سَمِعَ

فِي غُرْفَةِ ٱلْمُدِيرِ ؟– هُوَ سَمِعَ هُنَاكَ أَنَّكَ مَرِيضٌ

٣. أُخْتِي أَخَذَتِ ٱللَّحْمَ وَقَسَمَتْهُ إِلَى قِسْمَيْنِ   ٤. أَيْنَ

ٱلْكِتَابُ ٱلْجَدِيدُ ٱلَّذِي ٱشْتَرَيْتُهُ فِي ٱلدُّكَّانِ

ٱلْجَدِيدِ ؟– أُخْتُكَ وَضَعَتْهُ عَلَى ٱلْمَائِدَةِ ٱلْجَدِيدَةِ

٥. بَقَرَتَاكِ أَسْمَنُ مِنْ بَقَرَتَيْ جَدَّتِي   ٦. بَيْتَاهُ أَقْرَبُ

مِنْ بَيْتَيْكَ   ٧. لِي كِتَابَانِ جَدِيدَانِ وَلَهُ أَيْضًا كِتَابَانِ

جَدِيدَانِ   ٨. أَيْنَ ٱلْحِمَارَانِ ؟– هُمَا فِي ٱلْبُسْتَانِ   ٩. أَيْنَ

بَيْتَا ٱلْخَيَّاطِ ٱلْجَدِيدَانِ ؟– هُمَا فِي ٱلسُّوقِ ٱلْجَدِيدِ

١٠. لَنَا ثَوْرَانِ وَلَهَا أَيْضًا ثَوْرَانِ   ١١. حِمَارَايَ أَكْبَرُ

مِنْ حِمَارَيْ أَخِي   ١٢. مَتَى زَارَ مُعَلِّمُكَ خَالَنَا ؟– هُوَ

زَارَهُ بَعْدَ ٱلظُّهْرِ   ١٣. جَدَّتُهَا زَارَتِ ٱلْيَوْمَ أُمَّ ٱلْمُعَلِّمِ

١٤. أَيْنَ تَعَلَّمْتَ ٱللُّغَةَ ٱلْعَرَبِيَّةَ ؟– تَعَلَّمْتُهَا فِي ٱلْمَدْرَسَةِ

Thirty-eighth Lesson

1. The Moslems do not drink wine and do not eat pork
2 The teachers and the lady-teachers of my school (in Arabic: the teachers of my school and its lady-teachers.) have visited in the afternoon the mosque which is in the quarter of the blacksmiths
3. Where did thy (m) brother learn the Arabic language ?— My brother learned the Arabic language in the school which is in the Jaffa street **4.** Hast thou (m.) learned the English language at school ?— Yes I have learned it there **5.** What are the four directions ?— The four directions are : East, West, North and South
6. What hast thou (m.) learned at school to-day ?— I have learned the four directions to-day **7.** Thy teachers have visited the teachers of my brother in the school **8.** Where is the little brother of the neighbour ?— He is now playing in front of the garden and is shouting in a loud voice **9.** Who shouted in front of the house in the forenoon ? — The little brother of the neighbour played and shouted in front of the house **10.** These teachers have been to-day in the forest and those teachers have been to-day in Jaffa **11.** My brother learned the Arabic and the English languages at school. **12.** Where is thy (m.) dog now ?— it is now in the room of grand-mother **13.** The teachers and the lady-teachers have been in Jerusalem to-day. **14.** Where are the lady-teachers of this school ?— They (f.) are in the vineyard of my grand-mother.

١. إِبْنِي كَانَ ٱلْيَوْمَ فِي ٱلْمَدْرَسَةِ ٱلَّتِي فِي شَارِعِ
يَافَا ٢. عَمُّنَا كَانَ ٱلْيَوْمَ فِي ٱلْقُدْسِ وَمُعَلِّمِي أَيْضاً
كَانَ هُنَاكَ ٣. أَيْنَ أُخْتِي ٱلصَّغِيرَةُ ٱلْآنَ؟ — هِيَ تَلْعَبُ
أَمَامَ ٱلْجَامِعِ ٤. هٰذَا ٱلشَّارِعُ أَطْوَلُ مِنْ ذٰلِكَ
ٱلشَّارِعِ ٥. ٱلْخَبَّازُونَ كَانُوا ٱلْيَوْمَ فِي بُسْتَانِ ٱلْجَدِّ
٦. مَنْ رَأَى ٱلْخَيَّاطِينَ ٱلْيَوْمَ؟ — أَنَا رَأَيْتُ ٱلْخَيَّاطِينَ
بَعْدَ ٱلظُّهْرِ ٧. مُعَلِّمُوا هٰذِهِ ٱلْمَدْرَسَةِ كَانُوا ٱلْيَوْمَ

فِي كَرْمِ أَخِي ٨. تَعَلَّمْتُ ٱللُّغَةَ ٱلْإِنْـكِلِيزِيَّةَ فِي

هَذِهِ ٱلْمَـدْرَسَةِ ٩. أَيْنَ تَعَلَّمَ ٱبْنُكَ ٱللُّغَةَ ٱلْعَرَبِـيَّةَ ؟ –

هُوَ تَعَلَّمَ ٱللُّغَةَ ٱلْعَرَبِـيَّةَ فِي يَافَا ١٠. مُدِيرُ هَذِهِ

ٱلْمَـدْرَسَةِ وَمُعَلِّمُوهَا رَجَعُوا ٱلْيَوْمَ مِنَ ٱلْقُدْسِ

Lesson 42

1. Where are the newspapers which I have bought in the forenoon ? — They are on my table   2. Where hast thou (m.) bought these new copy-books ?— I have bought them in the new shop   3. Take this chalk and draw a man on the blackboard 4. The blackboard is black and the chalk is white· 5. One ship of the ships which I saw in the morning has sunk in the afternoon   6. The bear is bigger than the wolf and the elephant is bigger than the bear 7. I have seen to-day the pupils of this school in the forest which is near Jaffa   8. When didst thou (m.) buy these books ?— I bought them last year. 9. For how much (money) did the farmer sell the fox and for how much (money) did he buy the ass ?— The farmer sold the fox for one Palestinian pound and bought the ass for two Palestinian pounds   10. This merchant and his partner opened a new shop in the new market   11. The partners of this company are richer than the partners of that company   12. These hares are bigger than those hares 13. The houses in this street are bigger than the houses (that are) in that street   14. I have seen to-day the pupils of this school in the large forest which is near Haifa.

Lesson 43

1. The farmer have sown to-day turnip in the garden   2. The landlord has been to-day in the village and has bought there for one Palestinian pound straw from the farmers. 3. These pupils are diligent and those (pupils) are lazy   4. These schools are larger than those (schools). 5. Where didst thou (m.) leave the dogs of my grand-father?— I left them in the vineyard. 6. These houses are larger than the houses in that street   7. When hast thou (m.) bought these cocks ?— I bought them yesterday   8. What has Ibrahim drawn in the new copy-book ? — He has drawn there straight lines ° 9. This line is longer than all the other lines   10. The sons of the neighbour are lazy and his daughters are diligent 11. The daughters of my brother have learned in this school and his sons have learned in the school which is in the old city 12. The farmers who went out from the mosque went to Jaffa

13 From where did the pupils who have now entered the school return ?— They retuned from the forest   14.   What has the director of the school given to the pupils?— He has given them new books   15. These copy-books are dear. They are dearer than those copy-books   16. The sugar which I have bought in this shop is dearer than the sugar which I have bought in the market.

١. هٰؤُلَاءِ ٱلْفَلَّاحُونَ أَغْنَى مِنْ أُولَائِكَ ٱلْفَلَّاحِينَ

٢. أَيْنَ ٱشْتَرَيْتُمْ هٰذِهِ ٱلْكُتُبَ ٱلْجَدِيدَةَ ؟— أَنَا ٱشْتَرَيْتُهَا فِي ٱلدُّكَّانِ ٱلْجَدِيدِ   ٣. هٰؤُلَاءِ ٱلتَّلَامِيذُ كَسْلَانُونَ وَأُولَائِكَ ٱلتَّلَامِيذُ مُجْتَهِدُونَ   ٤. صَاحِبُ هٰذِهِ ٱلْبُيُوتِ غَنِيٌّ . هُوَ أَغْنَى مِنْ صَاحِبِ تِلْكَ ٱلْبُيُوتِ   ٥. أَيْنَ كِلَابُ ٱلْجَدِّ ؟— هِيَ فِي بُسْتَانِ ٱلْجَارِ

٦. تَلَامِيذُ هٰذِهِ ٱلْمَدْرَسَةِ كَانُوا ٱلْيَوْمَ فِي ٱلْغَابَةِ وَتَلَامِيذُ تِلْكَ ٱلْمَدْرَسَةِ كَانُوا هُنَاكَ ٱلْبَارِحَ

٧. أَلْبَيْتُ ٱلْجَدِيدُ أَكْبَرُ مِنَ ٱلْبَيْتِ ٱلْقَدِيمِ

٨. أَخِي بَاعَ بَيْتَهُ ٱلْقَدِيمَ وَٱشْتَرَى بَيْتًا جَدِيدًا

٩. رَأَيْتُ ٱلْبَارِحَ دُبًّا كَبِيرًا فِي قَفَصٍ   ١٠. ٱلْمَدَارِسُ فِي هٰذِهِ ٱلْقَرْيَةِ صَغِيرَةٌ . هِيَ أَصْغَرُ مِنَ ٱلْمَدَارِسِ فِي تِلْكَ ٱلْقَرْيَةِ

١١. هٰذِهِ ٱلدَّفَاتِرُ أَرْخَصُ مِنْ تِلْكَ ٱلدَّفَاتِرِ   ١٢. هٰذِهِ ٱلْبُيُوتُ ٱلْجَدِيدَةُ أَصْغَرُ مِنْ تِلْكَ ٱلْبُيُوتِ ٱلْقَدِيمَةِ   ١٣. هٰؤُلَاءِ ٱلْخَبَّازُونَ أَغْنِيَاءُ . هُمْ أَغْنَى مِنْ أُولَائِكَ ٱلْخَبَّازِينَ .

Lesson 46   1. What is there on the table ?— On the table there are books, copy-books and newspapers   2. We have drunk coffee in big cups and they (m.) have drunk coffee in small cups   3. What didst thou (m.) buy in the new shop ?— I bought there newspapers, copy-books and books   4. A thief entered the room of my big brother and stole the clock which my brother bought yesterday   5. I have written to-day with blue ink and my sister has written with red ink   6. My brother was in the magistrate's court (in Arabic . court of peace) and there saw the advocate who was yesterday in the vineyard of my grand-father. 7. Who has seen my new house ?— My mother saw it yesterday. 8 Thy father said that he waited for thee (m.) in the magistrate's court 9. The tailor waited for thee (m.) in the forenoon in his shop which is in the Moslem quarter. 10· Where is the cheese which I have bought in the market ?— It is in the kitchen   11. I have bought to-day in the market apples, grapes and nuts   12. This apple is sour and that apple is sweet   13. This nut is bigger than that nut.

١. هٰذِهِ ٱلسَّاعَةُ أَكْبَرُ مِنَ ٱلسَّاعَةِ ٱلَّتِي ٱشْتَرَاهَا

أَخُوكَ فِي ٱلْقُدْسِ ٢. أَيْنَ ٱلْجُبْنَةُ ٱلَّتِي وَضَعْتُهَا عَلَى

ٱلْمَائِدَةِ ؟— هِيَ عَلَى ٱلْمَائِدَةِ فِي ٱلْمَطْبَخِ ٣. هٰذَا

ٱلتُّفَّاحُ حَامِضٌ. هُوَ أَحْمَضُ مِنْ ذٰلِكَ ٱلتُّفَّاحِ

٤. مَنْ رَأَى ٱلْيَوْمَ مُدِيرَ هٰذِهِ ٱلْمَدْرَسَةِ ؟— أَنَا رَأَيْتُهُ

ٱلْيَوْمَ ٥. هٰذَا ٱلْبَيْتُ ٱلْجَدِيدُ أَصْغَرُ مِنْ بَيْتِ

ٱلْعَمِّ ٱلْقَدِيمِ ٦. مَا ٱشْتَرَى أَخُوكَ فِي ٱلدُّكَّانِ

ٱلْجَدِيدِ ؟— هُوَ ٱشْتَرَى هُنَاكَ كُتُبًا وَدَفَاتِرَ ٧. ٱلْبُيُوتُ

فِي هٰذِهِ ٱلْقَرْيَةِ أَكْبَرُ مِنْ بُيُوتِ تِلْكَ ٱلْقَرْيَةِ

٨. لِي كَلْبٌ أَبْيَضُ وَكَلْبٌ أَسْوَدُ. أَلْكَلْبُ ٱلْأَبْيَضُ

أَسْمَنُ مِنَ ٱلْكَلْبِ ٱلْأَسْوَدِ ٩. مَنْ رَأَى أَحْمَدَ

ٱلْيَوْمَ؟ ـ أُخْتِي رَأَتْهُ فِي ٱلسُّوقِ ٱلْجَدِيدِ ١٠. إِبْرَاهِيمُ

أَكْبَرُ مِنْ أَحْمَدَ وَأَحْمَدُ أَكْبَرُ مِنْ سَلِيمٍ ١١. أَبِي

كَانَ ٱلْبَارِحَ فِي حَقْلِ إِبْرَاهِيمَ

Lesson 49
1. The father of my father and the father of my mother are my grand-fathers (dual). The mother of my father and the mother of my mother are my grand-mothers (dual) and I am their (m.) grand-son   2. What has thy (m.) grand-father planted in your (m.) garden to-day? — My grand-father has planted date-palms in our garden to-day 3. Salim and his father went out from the magistrate's court and returned to their (dual) house which is in the old city 4. Salma and her mother have been in the mosque to-day. 5. My father and my mother are my parents (dual) and I am their (dual) son. My parents (dual) have other sons and daughters. Their (dual) sons are my brothers and their (dual) daughters are my sisters 6. My brother has been once in Jerusalem and twice in Haifa 7. My sister has been to-day in the zoo and there saw various vultures. 8. What is the thing that the old man has carried from the forest? — The old man has carried a bundle of fire-wood from there 9. Where are the new books which thou (m.) didst buy yesterday? — My big (elder) brother took them 10. My teachers and thine (m.) have been to-day in the Moslem quarter. 11. The daughters of our neighbour and his sons have been to-day in the forest which is near our village   12. Where are thy (m.) two new books and where are my two copy-books? — My two new books are in my room and thy (m.) two copy-books also are there.

Lesson 50
1. How many times has thy (m.) big (elder) brother been in Jaffa to-day? — My big brother has been there twice to-day   2. This hunter has hunted two hares to-day and slaughtered one of them (dual) and sold its meat in the market 3. This hunter always hunts in the forest which is near your (m.) village   4. Why does the child weep and (why do) the tears run from his eyes (dual)? — He weeps because of the glacial (in Arabic: of the strength of) cold. 5. Thy (m.) pupil came to me and after he saluted me said that thou (m.) didst wait for me in thy (m.) new house   6. The teacher of Zayd passed by my father and saluted him 7. Thy (m.) uncle

(on the father's side) has visited me yetserday and I shall visit him to-morrow, God willing!   8. When will thy (m.) uncle (on the mother's side) visit me ? — He will visit thee (m.) in the afternoon, God willing ! 9. Thy (m.) teachers have visited my teachers in the school to-day 10. Thy (m.) new houses are larger than their (m.) new houses   11. Who saw my two new houses ?— I saw them (dual)   12. The two dogs of my brother are bigger than thy (m.) two dogs.

١. كِتَابَاهُ ٱلْجَدِيدَانِ فِي غُرْفَتِي ٱلصَّغِيرَةِ ٢. أَيْنَ كَلْبَانَاهُ—هُمَا فِي غُرْفَةٍ جَدِّنَا ٣. كَمْ كِتَابًا ٱشْتَرَى أَبُوكَ ٱلْبَارِحَ فِي ٱلدُّكَّانِ ٱلْجَدِيدِ ؟—أَبِي ٱشْتَرَى ٱلْبَارِحَ كِتَابَيْنِ ٤. كَمْ أَرْنَبًا صَادَ ٱلصَّيَّادُ ٱلْبَارِحَ فِي هٰذِهِ ٱلْغَابَةِ ؟—هُوَ صَادَ ٱلْبَارِحَ أَرْنَبَيْنِ ٥. أَخُوهُ زَارَنِي ٱلْبَارِحَ وَأَنَا سَأَزُورُهُ بَعْدَ ٱلظُّهْرِ ٦. أَيْنَ دَفْتَرَايَ ؟— أَخُوكَ أَخَذَهُمَا ٧. مَنْ رَأَى ٱلْيَوْمَ حِمَارَيْ جَدِّي ؟— أَخُو جَارِنَا رَآهُمَا ٨. مُعَلِّمُوا ٱلْمَدْرَسَةِ ٱلْجَدِيدَةِ زَارُوا ٱلْيَوْمَ مُعَلِّمِينَا ٩. هٰتَانِ ٱلْبَقَرَتَانِ أَسْمَنُ مِنْ بَقَرَتَيْنَا ١٠. حِصَانَانَا أَكْبَرُ مِنْ حِصَانَيْكُمْ ١١. كَمْ دَفْتَرًا ٱشْتَرَى أَخُوكَ بَعْدَ ٱلظُّهْرِ ؟— هُوَ ٱشْتَرَى دَفْتَرَيْنِ ١٢. أُخْتُنَا أَكْبَرُ مِنْ أُخْتِكُمْ وَأُخْتُكُمْ أَكْبَرُ مِنْ أُخْتِهِ

Lesson 53

1. My cow is bigger than thy (m.) cow. It is the biggest cow in this village. 2. I have two red cows and thou (m.) hast two black cows ● 3. My neighbour has slaughtered to-day two lambs and distributed the meat gratis among the poor of this quarter 4. Our neighbour opened a fish-shop in the market which is in the old city 5. These children are dumb and those (children) are deaf. 6 Our neighbour has a big and fat ox. It is the biggest and fattest (ox) in our village. 7. My brother Ibrahim learns in the new school. He is the smallest pupil in it 8. My big brother has two big automobiles. He bought them (dual) last year in Jerusalem 9. The lessons in this book are easy and the lessons in that book are difficult 10. These lessons are easier than those (lessons) 11. This chair is heavy and that chair is light 12. This chair is heavier than that (chair). 13. That chair is lighter than this (chair) 14. I have a new house and my brother has a new house. The house of my brother is newer than my house 15. The two dumb sisters of our neighbour have visited to-day my big sister.

١. جَمَلاهُ أَكْبَرُ مِنْ جَمَلَيْنَا ٢. حِصَانُنَا هُوَ ٱلْحِصَانُ ٱلْأَكْبَرُ فِي هٰذِهِ ٱلْقَرْيَةِ. ٣. إِشْتَرَى أَخِي ٱلْبَارِحَ بَقَرَتَيْنِ بَيْضَاوَيْنِ ٤. هٰـتَانِ ٱلْبَقَرَتَانِ ٱلْبَيْضَاوَانِ سَمِينَتَانِ ٥. هٰذَا ٱلتِّلْمِيذُ كَسْلَانُ وَذٰلِكَ ٱلتِّـلْمِيذُ مُجْـتَهِدٌ ٦. لِي حِبْرٌ أَحْمَرُ وَلَهَا حِبْرٌ أَزْرَقُ ٧. أَيْنَ اشْتَرَى صَدِيقُكَ ٱلْحِبْرَ ٱلْأَحْمَرَ ؟ ـ هُوَ ٱشْتَرَى ٱلْحِبْرَ ٱلْأَحْمَرَ فِي ٱلدُّكَّانِ ٱلْجَدِيدِ ٨. ٱلدُّرُوسُ ٱلْيَوْمَ صَعْبَةٌ ٩. هٰذِهِ ٱلدُّرُوسُ أَسْهَلُ مِنْ تِلْكَ ٱلدُّرُوسِ ١٠. مَنْ فَتَحَ هٰذَا ٱلشُّبَّاكَ ٱلْـكَـبِيرَ ؟ ـ تِـلْمِيذُ أَخِي فَتَحَهُ ١١. أَيْنَ ٱلْبَقَرَةُ ٱلْبَيْضَاءُ ٱلَّـتِي ٱشْتَرَيْتُهَا ٱلْبَارِحَ ؟ ـ

اَلْبَقَرَةُ ٱلْبَيْضَاءُ فِي بُسْتَانِ جَدِّكَ .12 هَذِهِ ٱلْمَائِدَةُ

ثَقِيلَةٌ وَتِلْكَ ٱلْمَائِدَةُ خَفِيفَةٌ .13 تِلْكَ ٱلْمَائِدَةُ أَخَفُّ مِنْ

هَذِهِ ٱلْمَائِدَةِ .14 هَذِهِ ٱلْمَائِدَةُ أَثْقَلُ مِنْ تِلْكَ ٱلْمَائِدَةِ

Lesson 56

1. My elder brother has two big cars one of them (dual) is a passenger-car and the other is a transport-car   2. In the week there are 7 days and they are as follows: Sunday, Monday, Tuesday, Wednesday, Thursday, Friday and Saturday 3. In the day there are 24 hours; in the hour there are 60 minutes; in the $\frac{1}{2}$ hour there are 30 minutes; in the $\frac{1}{4}$ hour there are 15 minutes and in the $\frac{1}{3}$ hour there are 20 minutes. As to the minute it has 60 seconds   4. In each Palestinian pound there are 100 piastres and in each piastre 10 mils   5. For how much (money) hast thou (m.) bought fo-day apples and for how much (money) hast thou (m.) bought grapes?— I have bought to-day apples for 7 piastres and grapes for 13 piastres 6. For how much (money) didst thou (m.) buy these two copy-books? I bought one of them (dual) for 6 mils and the other (I bought) for 20 mils   7. How old art thou (m.)? — I am 15 years old   8. I am 25 years old and my elder brother is 33 years old   9. I have bought 4 new books to-day and my brother has bought 12 books 10. My little brother was in Jaffa twice, in Haifa 4 times and in Jerusalem 12 times.

Page 136

1. In this street there are 25 houses and in that street there are 27 houses 2. Where hast thou (m.) learned the Arabic language? —I have learned it in an evening school   3. In this town there are 4 evening schools for teaching the labourers reading and writing   4. Does this farmer know the reading and the writing? — No, this farmer does not know reading nor writing. He is illiterate.

5. Ahmad, read what I have written on the blackboard
6. The teacher said to his pupil : Ibrahim, read what
Zayd has written on the blackboard 7. In this evening
school there are 56 pupils 8. The wife of our neighbour does not know (the) reading nor (the) writing.
She is illiterate 9. The husband of this woman
learns the Arabic language in one of the evening
schools 10. My father has 12 cows and 5 camels.

١. كَمْ تِلْمِيذاً فِي هٰذِهِ ٱلْمَدْرَسَةِ ؟ ـ فِي هٰذِهِ ٱلْمَدْرَسَةِ
أَرْبَعَةٌ وَتِسْعُونَ تِلْمِيذاً ٢. لِجَدَّتِي ثَلَاثَةُ كِلَابٍ
كَبِيرَةٍ وَلِخَالِي كَلْبَانِ ٣. فِي هٰذَا ٱلْكِتَابِ سِتُّونَ
دَرْساً وَفِي ذٰلِكَ ٱلْكِتَابِ سَبْعَةٌ وَسِتُّونَ دَرْساً
٤. فِي هٰذِهِ ٱلْغُرْفَةِ أَرْبَعَةُ شَبَابِيكَ وَفِي غُرْفَةِ أُخْتِي
ثَلَاثَةُ شَبَابِيكَ ٥. إِشْتَرَيْتُ بَعْدَ ٱلظُّهْرِ خَمْسَةَ كُتُبٍ
فِي ٱلدُّكَّانِ ٱلْجَدِيدِ ٧. إِنْ كَمْ أَخُو جَارِنَا؟ ـ هُ
ٱبْنُ تِسْعَ عَشْرَةَ سَنَةً ٩. كَمْ مَرَّةً كَانَ جَارُنَا فِي
يَافَا ؟ ـ هُوَ كَانَ هُنَاكَ مَرَّتَيْنِ أَوْ ثَلَاثَ مَرَّاتٍ
١١. فِي هٰذِهِ ٱلْقَرْيَةِ مَدْرَسَتَانِ مَسَائِيَّتَانِ

Lesson 58 1. The 10th lesson in this book is easier
than the 16th lesson and the 53rd lesson
is more difficult than the 11th lesson 2. This peasant
ploughed his field to-day from 5 o'clock in the morning
until 11 o'clock 3. My brother ploughs his field twice
every day, once (in Arabic: the first time) from 6 o'clock

in the morning and once (in Arabic, and the other time)
from 3 o'clock to 5 o'clock in the after=noon   4. A
society was founded in this town to combat illiterateness
6.6 The peasant bought in this shop a sickle and his
wife bought there a knife   7. This book is composed
of three parts. In the first part there are 225 pages,
in the second part there are 364 pages and in the
third part there are 286 pages.

١. كِتَابُ أَخِي مُؤَلَّفٌ مِنْ جُزْأَيْنِ فِي الْجُزْءِ الْأَوَّلِ
ثَلَاثُمِائَةٍ وَخَمْسٌ وَخَمْسُونَ صَفْحَةً وَفِي الْجُزْءِ الثَّانِي
أَرْبَعُمِائَةٍ وَتِسْعٌ وَثَلَاثُونَ صَفْحَةً   ٢. كُنْتُ الْبَارِحَ
فِي الْقُدْسِ مِنَ السَّاعَةِ الثَّامِنَةِ صَبَاحًا إِلَى السَّاعَةِ
الثَّالِثَةِ بَعْدَ الظُّهْرِ   ٣. الدَّرْسُ السَّادِسَ عَشَرَ فِي هٰذَا
الْكِتَابِ أَصْعَبُ مِنَ الدَّرْسِ السَّابِعِ وَالثَّلَاثِينَ
٥. مَتَى كَتَبَ أَخُوكَ دُرُوسَهُ الْعَرَبِيَّةَ ؟ – هُوَ كَتَبَهَا
مِنَ السَّاعَةِ السَّادِسَةِ إِلَى السَّاعَةِ الثَّامِنَةِ مَسَاءً ٧. أَيْنَ
الْجُزْءُ الثَّالِثُ مِنْ هٰذَا الْكِتَابِ؟ – هُوَ فِي غُرْفَةِ أُخْتِنَا
٨. مَا كَتَبَتْ أُخْتُكَ بَعْدَ الظُّهْرِ ؟ – هِيَ كَتَبَتِ الدَّرْسَ
السَّادِسَ عَشَرَ   ٩. هٰذَا الدَّرْسُ أَسْهَلُ مِنَ الدَّرْسِ
الثَّامِنِ وَالْعِشْرِينَ ١٠. كَمْ دَرْسًا فِي هٰذَا الْكِتَابِ؟ –
فِي هٰذَا الْكِتَابِ سَبْعَةٌ وَخَمْسُونَ دَرْسًا